MY STORY

MY STORY

A Christian Tale

Jasper

To order additional copies of this book, contact:
Xlibris
1-888-795-4274
www.Xlibris.com
Orders@Xlibris.com
734466

I had been under suspicion for several emails I had sent. I was considered a terrorist threat beginning in November 17, 2013 while a resident of Baytown, Texas. Now, however, after being in much prayer about this, I know that my Lord has separated me from this monitoring, has removed me from further monitoring by the police. I asked God to move this mountain from me. I believe in my heart that He has done this for me. I no longer feel like I am a threat to society, nor did I ever think that I was to begin with, but, was, in reality, only a paper tiger. This suspicion carried with it a term of one year to test to see if I had any malice connected with my emails. I did not hear from the police, but I felt their presence everywhere I traveled. When I made reference to this incident to the Harris County arrest records department in downtown Houston, my name did not appear anywhere. So, I concluded my fate was in the hand of my Father, the Lord, who is all-knowing as well as all-seeing.

My memory fails me. I am no longer able to recollect certain things I have heard before. Like names of people, places and things of my past. Certain names simply do not appear and require time to recall, but even through patience they do not surface. This, to me, is very disheartening and disappoints me. I have been left behind like this for years on end by people who go on with their lives without me. I was told I had a gift. The gift to remember everything I have seen and heard all of my life is no small thing... What is important to you may not be so important to me, and vice-versa. And, this is where the rub is.

Thinking that all of us are in the same boat, holding to the same values, and doing the same things every day, will not be a pleasant suitor. The idea of planning our days around our families and living life according to the traditions, every man's dream is to have a family of his own, but it wasn't for me. I can say this without looking beyond myself. I confess this is true. But, I will say, everyone will try to convince me that I have been a fool for not becoming even remotely interested in such a life like they have made for themselves. This is demonstrated, by default, of any other lifestyle that may be available. There is no other lifestyle but theirs to adhere to, for I am simply not living according to the interests and values outlined by normal people. This is very unnerving to go through life, thinking I was not made for any other purpose than to be ridiculed and shamed, beaten or abused for their enjoyment. And, they do not even attempt to recognize their faults, even to say 'it is no fault at all they have committed against me'. Insisting I have acted alone, without the consent of my parents, I have thought I had been raised by a pack of wild dogs. And, since I have been lucky to have survived this long, they would now consider my parents the ones who were wrong. I have got to forgive them because of health and emotional stability. And, my own experience of things, compared to how most people have experienced the same things, is true, that my views of things are, indeed, adolescent, in relation to theirs, which takes on an adult nature. This is not an opinion, but a fact, based on biological evidence from my birth.

My birth was indeed a controversial one. The facts I have are derived from looking at my birth certificate. It says I was born dead, while above these words, "born alive" are written. Born dead is interesting because my mother's notes indicate I stopped eating while in her fifth month of pregnancy. This would be the month when a baby would become stillborn. I had not been taking any food. My mother's notes indicated she did not gain a pound while in this fifth month, so I concluded that during this month is when I actually died. This is based on the knowledge I have gained as a result of hearing other stories of babies being born with encephalitis, an enlarged brain. An enlarged brain can be caused by an injection of fluoride while the mother is in her early stages. The research of my mother's notes indicates at the end of her third month this injection was given to her, unbeknownst to her. Can this happen that a mother would not be informed? I say, of course, she can be in the dark, if there is a plan already in place by the doctor and my dad. Why, you ask? Because my mother would go to her next month's check-up insisting the doctor know I was kicking too much, that she was very concerned. While telling the doctor this, he would laugh it off and tell her not to worry, but that I would come to term as planned. Well, I did come to term, but not after I had died, following this kicking episode. Why do I say this is true? Because, like I noted before, I had stopped taking food from my mother in her fifth month. She did not gain any weight. I kicked too much, my mother said. Can you imagine having your brain balloon up to a size bigger than normal and then, trying to alert someone to help save your life the only way I knew how? The only way was to kick my mother's stomach. I was going through a very frightening nightmare and I felt very helpless and powerless to stop it. And, then the roof fell in, so to speak.

I was hospitalized in the early 1990's for claustiphobia and was confined to a psyche ward. I was around the age of 45 years old then. Can we see a connection here between birth and real life later in my life, living out my birth again and again after becoming an adult?

Somehow, after this fifth month, I came back to life. I made it to the ninth month, delivered on January 3, 1952 in Amarillo, Texas. I resumed taking food and was no longer dead. How this occurred I may never know. Both of my parents have since died, as well as the doctor, I presume. I was administered hypnosis back in the early 1980's for a treatment I knew nothing about, except that I had just spent 12 weeks confined in a facility that treated various mental problems. The staff in the hospital told me nothing about the reasons I was there. They went ahead and gave me medications on my first night there. I did not like this at all because I had always prided myself on taking care of myself. I never liked to take medicine for anything, especially if I did not know what I was taking them for. All I knew, was when I signed up for the Armed Forces in downtown Houston, the lady who took my application mentioned to someone there at the counter about a "mental institution", and I overheard it. I prepared to fill out my application. This was around the year 1979 or 1980. I did recall having thoughts about mental institutions before that day I overheard her mention it. So, it was not something new for me to hear. And, besides, my dad had been in a mental institution when I was 12 years old. He told me never to tell anybody about this, rain or shine. It was a secret. Believe me, I never did mention it to anyone. I was scared what would happen if I did mention it to anybody. Not until I had been in a mental facility myself, practically 16 years after he had came back from his interment, did I realize it might be okay to spill the beans. As inheriting genes would be from my mother and dad at the outset would make me crazy someday, this is what I thought I was in this mental facility for. Yes, I did think often about heredity. I could not stop heredity, but learned that it was inevitable, like an obstacle I would not be able to overcome. If you have ever been in this type of situation, then you know it is a very unpleasant thing to go through.

I went to Sunday school one Sunday and told one person there about being confined and he relayed the message to someone else. I didn't really care that he would tell anybody else anymore. I would not feel guilty either about sharing the truth that my dad had been in a mental institution. No one knew about it, that I had been there or that my dad had earlier been there, so the veil had been lifted from my shoulders to speak openly about it and not fear being judged because of it. I had been going to that Sunday school every Sunday prior to becoming hospitalized. I had sung solos and had been a member of the youth choir and had been a part of revivals the youth pastor would take us on.

I was given the opportunity to masturbate at the same age of 12 because my family had just sterilized me. Because I could not have children in my future, they made it possible for this to happen. A Sunday school teacher told me so when I was age 15; never to touch a girl or kiss a girl. So, I was adept at finding pornography magazines and materials to masturbate with when I had the urges. I even found the XXX movie theaters in town to go to. I wanted to keep this as secret as possible because I was not proud of this behavior at all, especially when I knew my friends were all going out and having fun on weekends. They were making plans to get married and going on with their lives and careers and I was sick about this to the point of taking my own life.

Encephalitis would ensure I would enter the mental health system and stay in it for the rest of my life. My dad has been dead for 16 years, so he is not around to answer my question. I do know, however, I got up this morning by the grace of God, fully aware of His presence, after praying at my bedside last night on my knees. I had a disagreement with the cook and the staff member at dinner time last evening after I was refused service for a cup of iced coffee.

My mind was going through the law of diminishing returns from day one. As a result, I became deeply depressed. Because of the abandonment I felt from my friends, they were going on with their lives and I wasn't. Being born with encephalitis guaranteed mental illness later on when I was about 35 years old. And, it did come true, against my better will. A deteriorating mind is what I inherited from the time of my birth. That is the hand I drew. A mind that started out at 100% and deteriorated on a minute-by-minute basis for the rest of my natural-born life. Encephalitis is an enlarged brain brought on by a manipulative father and a doctor who went along with the intentions of my father. But, my first look at my baby picture in my mother's arms was that my head was of a normal size. This tells me that the enlargement process did not manifest itself until about two to three years after my birth. I noticed a sharp difference in the size of my brain in a picture that was taken when I was about two and one half years old. In that picture, my forehead was extended beyond normal size. My head extended to a measure of two or three inches outward, in front. The backside of my head was almost razor thin and slick, straight up and down. By the time I was about 4 years old, my mother would take pictures in the winter time to disguise my brain size. She adorned my head with a big cap, covering my head from top to bottom so anyone who looked would not be able to distinguish the oversized brain. I think my dad and mom planned it this way when they left the house with me so no one would be talking about them. The consequences of their actions would be compromised and they would not be fingered for doing something illegal. This is something akin today to the action of abortion, killing babies, and a form of genocide.

This case was real because it was the end of a family tree. I think my mother held it against my dad because my mother knew she could have raised a good boy to be a proper father and husband like any other boy. She felt that this was premature reasoning on the part of my dad that he did not take into account how good a mother and wife he had married to bring up a child who could be a good father. He underestimated what God could have done in my life and the power my mother, his wife, had in raising me to be a good father and husband.

I once made a snowman out of real snow. It was in my hometown of Guymon, Oklahoma. I was about 9 years old. I did not finish it, though. I went inside to ask my mom for the eyes made of coal and the nose, but she did not have any of those things.

I lived in a halfway house for 12 years. I lived with other mental patients. I did not commit a crime to be put into this place. I simply needed a roof over my head when I was laid off from my job and I could not pay my rent without an income. I notified my doctor and he is the one who put me in there, almost immediately.

There were times when I would want to change my medication and there were things I did to make the owner of the house put me into the hospital. I wanted desperately to close out my drug habits and quit drinking and resume my life away from being addicted to street substances. And, I succeeded there in doing this. This is what the hospitalizations were for, to rid me of this craving for medicating the pain I had experienced from a life of not receiving the attention I needed. As long as I took my medications, the owner would not consider hospitalizing me. I could, though, decline to eat and it would not cause such a big stir as declining medications. And, there were times I fasted and prayed alongside my bed as well as praying at my bedside in the hospital.

November 17th, 2014 has come and gone. One year has passed since the start of my no-trespass order that was handed down by the Baytown Police Department. I presume all is well with my case.

I exited the halfway house of Houston's southwest side in June of 1999 after getting employment through Goodwill Industries' main campus. Mr. Bill Lufburrow's group there made me apply by filling out an application. Then, I went in for an interview and they put me to work as a cashier/clerk on the staff at the Hwy. 290/34th Street Goodwill store. Mrs. Dee Hawkins secured a way for me to get to work every single day. Her friend, a preacher, donated a car to her for me to use once the rides she would provide for me, would end. This preacher led me to his antique business one day and then, told me that I would have to drive myself back to his store by memory if I were to have the use of the car he was going to donate. It worked. My memory of how to get to his antique business worked. From there, I drove this little blue car every day to work until my dad bought for me a new car. Not a new car in years, but a Skylark, a 1992 Buick Skylark. It was a beautiful burgundy/red, a two-door sedan my dad bought at Strickland Chevrolet in Pearland, Texas. My dad had a friend at Strickland whose name was Martin Williamson, a salesman there. Mr. Williamson said he had one car that had just come in to his dealership from an elderly couple who had driven all the way from Indiana overnight. He said the car had overheated when they arrived in Houston, so they dropped it off at Strickland and while there they also bought a new car from Martin. He said before I would buy this Skylark, he would send it to the maintenance shop to have the transmission overhauled free of charge so that the car would no longer overheat. My dad agreed with this and I was glad too, because when we took it out on the road for a test drive, this Skylark almost didn't make it back to Strickland. It started to overheat right away, so my Uncle Rondall, out to visit my mom, his sister, from California, suggested we stop at a local maintenance shop where the mechanics could look at the car and tell us what in the world was wrong with this car. So, we did. And, the mechanic in charge told my Uncle Rondall about the car and Rondall told the salesman, Martin Williamson, what the mechanic at this shop told him. This is how my car became fixed before I even drove it out of the dealership. Strickland Chevrolet spent around $4,000 on fixing the problem on the transmission. The car cost my dad around $4,000 which he said he would put on his credit card for me. Rondall, my mom, my dad, and I all went to a local fast food restaurant for a meal while waiting for Strickland to fix my car. This was a very nice and pleasant day for me, looking forward to owning and driving my very own car again since I had to give up my 1978 Cutlass Supreme for $50. The Cutlass I brought with me to the Halfway House in 1985. My Cutlass was also a burgundy/red in color.

Mrs. Dee sent me to enroll in a business school downtown shortly after becoming a resident there with her. So, I drove my Cutlass downtown and parked in the garage every day. One day, it would not start when I put the key in the ignition, so I had to start walking home. About the time I crossed the Highway 59 highway interchange between downtown and the start of Richmond Avenue, a truck pulled up. I was walking on the right side of the road on Richmond. I knew him. He lived just across the street from the halfway house. He said, get in the truck and I'll take you home. He went to church every Sunday in his suit and tie. He lived alone but had a helper to keep his business going. He had a woodshed on his property too. He let me go in to it one time. He had family members over on Sundays a few times I was there for 12 years. They were all dressed up too, like they had just gone to church together and were getting together for a family reunion of sorts. He ended up buying my car for $50 because I did not have enough money to fix the problem. Eventually, my Cutlass came back to the property I lived on out of the garage downtown. My friend needed to secure the owner's title of my Cutlass before he would purchase it from me. So, I got in his car and he took me to the title shop and got a copy of it for his records to keep. I told him I did not know where my original title was since I had to come to the halfway house alone. And, a lot of my stuff from my previous apartment had gotten taken or stolen from me on arriving there. In fact, most of my stuff was not given back to me when I finally got moved in. Even my change I kept on my dresser disappeared rather quickly. I must have had change that amounted to a few dollars in a glass bowl. Whoever took the money left the bowl for me. My vacuum cleaner disappeared also. I brought all my stuff from my efficiency apartment out in Kuykendall/Rankin

Road that day. A white van pulled up outside with a driver who would later become a resident at the halfway house also. He was a Moslem by faith and would do a lot of chores for Ms. Dee. He would be a painter who would paint a whole house I would later live in by myself. Inside and out, too. Even my figurines disappeared on that van when it pulled up to my brand new duplex in southwest Houston that day from Kuykendall/Rankin Road. My dinette set I bought a few years ago at Fingers Furniture on the Gulf Freeway went missing also. I guess there wasn't any room in the duplex for it. The duplex was a furnished duplex after all. But, Ms. Dee did use my phone, my princess phone. She mounted it on the wall by the door and kept my bill in her possession every month to pay for. She wired it from somewhere inside the apartment along the wall, It was a light blue princess phone, the color of the Houston Oilers.

So, I consider the Lord has delivered me from being held in suspicion over being a terrorist threat to society. The deadline of one year has passed, as of yesterday, the 17th day of November, 2013, the day the police of Baytown gave me this warning.

I am no longer welcome at Second Baptist Church, the church I attended for over 10 years in Houston, Texas. I went there to talk to someone about a shelter to move into but the person there said I would have needed to join in a program to be a part of the shelters on his list, so I departed. But, before I did, I wanted to check with Charlie Townsend of the Prayer Ministry, where I worked several years. When I tried to locate him at the Prayer Ministry, the Second Baptist Church security team met me outside and told me that I would have to leave the building premises. So, I did.

Dr. David Kaye died a few years ago in Houston. He was a good friend of mine in the Second Baptist church choir for several years. He was a psychiatrist in Houston and also had a radio show with KHCB as a Christian call-in counseling show. He advised me several different times on my medications and how to settle things on trying to rid myself of taking them in the future should I so choose to do so. He was from Illinois originally, Springfield, Illinois, to be exact.

Carol Morganti also used my princess phone one day while we were together in my apartment in Lubbock, Texas. I think it was the same color, blue, as my princess phone I had later had in Houston.

The song, the Long and Winding Road, by John Lennon of the Beatles, keeps coming up as a melody associated with meeting Carol. Also, the Whitney Houston song, "I'll always love you", also keeps coming up as a result of meeting Carol. I liked Roy Rogers and Dale Evans as a boy. I liked to listen to Gene Autry tunes on my record player. Rudolph the Red Nosed Reindeer was a favorite of mine. The Wabash Cannonball was another favorite. Secret Agent Man I also liked later in my teenage years.

Abraham, one of the clients at Dee's Halfway House, would put his feet on the dinner table when we would be eating. I could not believe this. I had never seen this before from anybody in my life. Sometimes, he wouldn't even wear shoes to the table to eat. I was told he was abused growing up, of having to be told to put his feet on the dining room table to eat his meals. I could not understand this at all when I heard this. He later died from smoking himself to death. Abraham would pick up cigarette butts off the ground and light them up, smoking sometimes only the filters. I could not get used to seeing Abraham do this. It would bother me to no end, why he would do such a thing every single day when everybody else was resting or taking some personal time by themselves. I wanted to tell Abraham he was killing himself, but deep in my heart I could not stop him if he so wanted to do this. One time, Ms. Dee wanted me to give Abraham a bath. And, so I did. I guess Abraham wasn't able to give himself a bath on his own. One guy, Juan Ramirez, out of prison I suppose, would drink a lot and his eyes would go back in his head. His eyes would go up, Ms. Dee said, so she told me several times to give Juan his medicine when this happened. And, I did. And, after several minutes, Juan's eyes would return to normal and he would walk out the house and go home, I suppose. I never knew where they would go. This would also bother me to no end. I would always be asking myself where they go when they walk out the door. One guy never came back. He overdosed on his medication, killing himself. I can still remember him walking out of the house that day he killed himself. I never talked to him. He never said a word the whole time I knew him there. That bothered me too, not that I was scared of him, but that, maybe I could have said something to halt his intention to kill himself. How did I know? I did not know what they were thinking.

Mike Wollard, another client at Dee's, told me on our way to Whataburger for a cup of coffee, there were zillions of cars out there. He was diabetic and had been such for the majority of his life. He began to regurgitate his food and had to be given over to a nursing home. Mike would later pass away shortly after entering the nursing home. He came back to Dee's one last time to eat dinner with us before he passed. I still miss Mike. He became a Christian there later on in our stay together. So, I guess I will be seeing Mike again when I also graduate from here.

Rhonda Davis was a girl who said she was the runner-up to Miss North Houston beauty contest one year. She said she lived in Acres Homes before she came to Dee's. Her father showed up one day at Dee's. And, he would look at me closely while he stood just inside the front door. Sylvester Lawson said she had been abused by her father, I presume, sexually molested as well. This is one reason she became mentally ill, I suppose. She was a gifted girl though. She said she made all A+'s in her school growing up. Most of the time she was real sweet but one day she stabbed me with a pencil.

I was selected the recipient of the Governor's Man Award for Key Clubs in the Texas/Oklahoma district in 1970. I was awarded the trophy at the Shamrock Hilton in Houston at our convention that was held every year in different locations throughout Texas and Oklahoma. I was given a huge ovation, I remember, because the delegation from my home club stood to cheer me when I came to the podium to receive my trophy. I just stood there and gave my thanks with the trophy in my right hand. It was the final award given at the convention. We had a contest among the lieutenant governors that year to see who could have the best presentation in their divisions to produce a week of activities and events to celebrate the country and patriotism of being an American citizen. Most of the other lieutenant governors would involve themselves in raising money through bake sales or concession stand revenues to boost their standing among the selection committee, who were responsible for picking the winner who would claim the Governor's Man Award that year at the convention. I, however, did not concern myself with raising money or getting myself or the club any attention, outside of honoring my country through a speech at the high school assembly hall, members taking over responsibility for raising the American flag every day at school, and several other events our club would do to honor our country without raising money for ourselves or anybody else. I believe this is how I was chosen to be the award winner.

I also was awarded the Most Outstanding Journalist award for the Panhandle of Texas that same year, 1970. I was a sports writer for my school's newspaper staff. I believe I was awarded this trophy mainly because I put together a sports brochure on behalf of my school that year. It was the very first sports brochure my school had ever had. Most of the other schools in our district had had their own sports brochures done for a long time. They would compile these for the use of the newspapers, radio sports shows, and other news outlets who could take advantage of the information.

I also won an award for acting. I played the role of Hartzell Spence in the play, One Foot in Heaven. I was awarded a little card with the inscription on it saying, Lead Actor in a One-Act play for UIL contestants, Canyon, Texas. I also was awarded All-Region Choir one year and I received a patch to go on a jacket. I was selected to lead my church choir as the minister of music when I was only 16 years old. It wasn't the biggest church in town, the second largest Baptist church, called Calvary Baptist Church. I don't know why my mom chose this church over the bigger Baptist church in town. Maybe, she thought I would have a better opportunity to demonstrate my musical talent in a smaller church. Anyway, Mrs. Stanley, I'll call her, bought a guitar for me to play. And, I brought it home. I couldn't play it because the beginner's book was too hard for me to figure out. I was lost trying to learn to play my brand new guitar. And, to make matters worse, my mom said she wasn't going to pay anybody to teach me to play. Mrs. Stanley wanted me to play in her Sunday school class soon after she bought this new guitar. So, I had to learn a song real fast, as good as I could muster until that Sunday morning rolled around in front of her young adult class. I survived it as well as I could, but this would be the last demonstration of my guitar playing talent for a while. And, it was, until someone loaned me a guitar while under the roof of Laurelwood Hospital in the Woodlands.

Mrs. Stanley also devised a plan for me to serve as leader of the church nursery for a period of time. Included in this deal was a pianist, a girl from an adjacent high school. Well, when I asked this girl out for a date, she flat refused me.

I am (Leslie Moorhead): Mr. Pembroke, the man with 5 different faces. Les, the boy who was a man dressed in a bow-tie; Les, the athlete stud little boy with the neck of a football player; little Leslie, the blockhead who sweats bullets. Leslie, the boy with buckteeth and the life of the party, who has a bruised fingernail on his left index finger. And, last, but not least, is look-alike Leslie, named Billy, who looks nothing like the other four Leslie's and Les's. Billy was referred to as Billy-goat by Mrs. Peterson, my second-grade teacher, who called me a Billy-goat. Her son, Kim, was the one who sent me to the emergency room one day to have three stitches put into the back of my head. Kim pushed me over the rail at school while I was talking to a girl. I don't remember the name of the girl.

This reminds me of another time when I received another set of stitches this time in my chin, in Corpus Christi, Texas. My friend, Rusty Cook and some other friends drove from Lubbock to Corpus where Rusty took us to Padre Island to surf. He told me how to get on the board and how to ride the surf wave. I did, however, the board flipped up and struck my chin which brought blood. Rusty's mother was called from the beach cabin and she came to take me to the doctor to stitch my chin up. On the way to Corpus that day, Rusty would direct me into his relative's living room to talk to a woman, whom he said was "crazy." So, I did, but I did not say anything to her. She was middle-age and she wasn't very attractive. I sat by her for a minute or two, but I soon got up.

But, as it says in the Bible, all things work together for good for those who are the called according to His purpose, and do according to His will the things He has purposed them to do from before the foundation of the world. Let it be so.

(Prayer): Dear Lord: You heard sounds of rebellion and blasphemy against your very name and your very character, as I also heard with my own opened ears you were miraculously opening for me to hear and witness here just a few minutes ago. The degradation of your name by these bullies who are murdering, stealing from, and envying at the same time, are bent on their own destruction. Why? Because they love the idea of death more than life. As you also heard and witnessed this debacle for the past hours, Satan devised a plan to end mine and your success and development of love in me as quickly as possible. Satan's plan unfolded according to his desires. I could see him designing and preparing to be victorious towards me, my Lord. Just like clockwork, like Satan works all his works. It went off, I saw, without a hitch. Satan involves himself in teaching God how to operate and counseling God on how to get the job done correctly. The only trouble is, Satan continues never to learn, by reason God placed in his heart, is that he always comes up a little short. God still owns the key to all of His creative order.

A gambler is Satan's calling card. Maynard G. Krebs, the name given to Dobie Gillis' best buddy, who also played Gilligan on Gilligan's Island. A thug, of sorts, whom Dobie always wanted to teach. Playing with people's emotions is what Maynard G. Krebs was accused of doing to his only friend, Dobie Gillis. Maynard made up stories he hoped Dobie would believe to bring pity and sympathy from good old friend, Dobie. Dobie wore many different hats and masks to hide his anger and resentment. His quality to be an expert on every issue, Maynard would bring to his attention. So, Dobie told Maynard he would have to wait until he came up with the perfect plan to solve Maynard's problem. It might take a while, he told Maynard. He also said to wait as long as it took for Dobie to return with a solution. He promised him an answer, but, in reality, was giving Maynard the run-around. Dobie made Maynard think he was less valuable to the human race than he perceived he was. Dobie perceived that he was better than Maynard. Maynard, once learning this, began to actually believe it was true of him. Being gullible is not so great a quality, is it?

James Jeter was a friend of mine. At the age of 15, I began my friendship with James. It was a strange one, to put mildly. It would have its ups and downs. James wanted desperately to be a good football player on the school team. He wanted to bulk up, so he would be strong enough to block the defensive guys opposite the line. He was the tight end on our starting offense. He trained hard by mixing eagle brand evaporated milk and another concoction to gain more muscle mass and to gain weight. He had a set of barbells in his bedroom and anytime he needed, he could get pumped up.

James was very popular at school. He was the student council vice-president and a finalist for class favorite. James enlisted me to come with him and his daddy on their morning runs to deliver soft drinks to grocery stores. It was a Coca-Cola delivery truck and James' dad was the distributer/driver. One day, James and I went alone, James driving his dad's truck while I helped him with the unloading, riding shotgun.

My mother's photo albums captured my attention one day. The pictures were taken of our next-door neighbors, the Jeters, when we were very young. The pictures gave the address of our duplex complex. It showed little James Jeter, and me, almost side-by-side. We met again almost 15 years later in a different town, this time, we were a little further apart in location, but I still could walk to the Jeter house in five minutes or less.

Without confession and humility toward God, we cannot enter His courts with thanksgiving and praise. Cleansing does not happen to our souls unless we confess our sins and own up to the wrongs we have done to others. There were so many secrets my dad would tell me to keep that I felt I couldn't open my mouth except to come to the table to eat my food for breakfast, lunch, and dinner. Otherwise, I was a prisoner in my own home. I was held from going to dances on weekends. I was asked to go to the prom one time and several cotillion dances also, I did not know how to dance very well but my dates would understand and try to help me learn. Back in Oklahoma, we had square dancing after school but I wasn't thrilled about learning that either. Texans did not square dance like Oklahomans did. Besides, my mother made it clear to me she did not want me to do what everybody else did anyway, including dancing.

I was invited to spend the night with James Jeter one summer. He and I got on a pallet of blankets next to his outside faucet and his dog, King, in his back yard. Well, King kept agitating James, so James devised a plan to get up and roam the neighborhood to wake Neal Derrick's family from their sleep. Neal was also on the football team, a defensive end. Neal liked to work on cars and he once told me he wanted to be an auto mechanic. We entered their carport that night late and made enough sounds and noise to wake the Derrick household up. The police were called to the Jeter residence and James disappeared while I sat in his front room listening to his father telling the police officer that his son, James, had nothing to do with this disturbance. In fact, Mr. Jeter would tell the officer it was my idea to go walking the neighborhood after 10:00 o'clock to wake up the Derrick family. The officer told me to get in his squad car while James stayed with his family at home. James never would speak to me about this night again, and I don't recall ever bringing it up to him either. The officer telephoned my dad, who was asleep, from the street in front of the Jeter household, to let him know that he was enroute to the police station for an investigation into the disturbance. The policeman asked me several questions and took each answer I gave him down on paper, and decided not to hold me in a jail cell that night, but warned me very severely not to do anything else like this again or I will end up in jail, for sure. My dad showed up a few minutes later and took me home and warned me about hanging around with the wrong crowd.

I would ride with James to the clothing store after his mother would give him a blank check to buy as many clothes as he wanted. I watched in total amazement each time this occurred. His salesperson would always be overjoyed to help assist James. James would leave with boxes of new clothes under his arms and I would help him carry them into his house. He did offer me a Mountain Dew one time out of his refrigerator, but, only if I would sit down with him at the table.

James' mother took me to her job one day to see her work. She was a bookkeeper. She usually wore black and she had a smoke habit, as did James' father. James' younger brother, Rusty, was shorter in height than his brothers, James and Gene. Rusty died young, at age 20 approximately, falling in a big oil drum some 300 feet below from the top stairwell. I last saw Rusty at college my sophomore year. He was actually a freshman student when we ran into each other. He had a big smile on his face. I will never forget that big smile. He liked Mick Jagger and the Rolling Stones. James informed me he had another sibling that was born before Rusty was born, but later died. Rusty's favorite song from the Stones' was "I can't get no satisfaction".

Carnal-minded people, together with spiritually-minded people, are a lesson in futility. I bear hard the teaching of God's word. I bear the burdens hard. It never gets any easier.

December 6, 2014

June Hunt met with my brother David in Lubbock to help direct the rest of my life's ministry of Jesus Christ. I never was fortunate enough to listen to her that day, and I am sorry I was never able to talk with her personally. I saw an appearance she made years later on television discussing her ministry. She still impressed me as I would listen to her live radio show. She became a very rich lady, I presume, being able to sell her products she composed on tapes, etc. I learned that her father, H. L. Hunt, was a good Christian man in the city of Dallas. June was his daughter from a second marriage. Mr. Hunt had a previous marriage that produced more children than the first marriage would. H. L. Hunt was the founder of the Hunt Oil Company. My brother David became acquainted with the Hunt family when David was a younger man. David was an accomplished pianist and vocalist and traveled with June on several mission trips around the world.

My parents put me through a tough period growing up, by separating themselves from each other twice. Legally separated, they called it then, even though I didn't remember anything about a paper being drawn up or anything like that. I was so confused and afraid they would divorce one another that I planned to escape any more trouble by running away from home. Something interrupted my plight, however. I had to go to the restroom. A case of the jitters was in the works that I had not planned on initially when I drew it up. So, mom made everything normal again by sending us to see Ben Hur, the movie at the drive-in. It was a four-hour movie. I fell asleep in the back seat soon after we parked our car. And, I did not wake up again until the final scene came when the chariot race was on.

Every man and beast and fowl and cow and creeping thing died in the flood. The flood waters were 15 cubits high and the mountains were covered. Only Noah and his family survived with the animals that were housed on the ark. The violence God saw on the earth, it repented the Lord that He had made man. And, He was grieved in His heart.

Ms. Dee's grandson threw rocks at me, covered my head with shave cream, while her other grandson would put me in a choke hold, wrestling-style, head-lock and wouldn't let me go until I begged. They say blood is thicker than water, so in this case, they might be right. For one thing, I was only one in a hand full of whites on the premises. The remaining people were black, maybe 15 or 20 of them. All I ever saw on a daily basis were black people, not whites. So, I began to subconsciously think I was black, not because I was jealous or felt less than them, but, because I was outnumbered. She had many supporters. She would always insist she loved Jesus. She prayed over our meals every time we sat down to eat, but in retrospect, these were so routine and became monotonous. She would thank God for the hands that prepared each meal, which was her. I would think she would save the best for last in each prayer, which would be to thank God, and herself.

Chris Hinchey was a friend of mine. We both lived in the same town but we did not attend the same schools. Chris was a rancher's son who managed an automobile dealership in this small town in Oklahoma.

Chris was an athlete like I was. He played football, basketball, and baseball like I did. Chris invited me to spend the night with him. He took me to his ranch and his daddy was baling hay. He had horses, too. When we retired for the evening, he pulled the covers over me and told me to listen, to hear the hyenas out in the pasture behind us. I asked him if they laughed like laughing hyenas do? I do not remember what his answer was.

Another friend of mine invited me to his farm/ranch to spend the night with him soon after Chris did. He actually let me get on one of his horses so I could know how it felt to ride a real horse. It was fantastic. I got him up to a gallop. I was only 11 or 12 years old but I had asked my dad if I could have my own horse, before and he said "no." So, this made me feel better. I do not remember what his name was, but I will always remember he let me ride and then, he would want to talk to me before we retired for the night. I remember he was very caring and talked with a smile.

Another friend of mine was Cheryl Sones. When I returned from Lubbock to Houston after I failed to finish my degree at Texas Tech University, I went to church with my mom at Park Place Baptist Church. It was in the college class that Cheryl and I met. She was tall and thin and had very long blondish hair that reached almost to her waist line. Her family lived in nearby Pasadena with her mother, father, and younger brother, Richard. She became my newest girlfriend. She was like a mother to all of us in the class. I would find her telephone number and I would call her several times. When I asked her to be my girlfriend, she turned me down. I cannot remember what her reason was except that she was seeing someone else at that time. I actually cried on the telephone when

I learned this and I told her I did not want to lose her. I even went to a jewelry store and bought her an engagement ring which was worth about $1,000. When I told my mother I had bought her the ring, she came unglued and told me we had to be engaged first and at least be dating. So, I returned the ring to the jewelry store, embarrassed and hurt again. The men at work would always tell me I had to talk to a girl. But, this time, as other times, it did not work. Cheryl went on to later marry another guy and I attended the wedding reception. I said to Cheryl, as I walked out, "and, they said it wouldn't last".

Tainted white is what I am now, knowing what I have been referred to all of my life, I just didn't know it until now. This is what the people who made the decision for me to be sterilized would refer to me as reason for this procedure to be carried out. As far as I have been known, and talked to other people for over 62 years, I am the only male I am aware of that was ever sterilized. This stands to reason because of the warnings I was issued from very early on in my childhood. Although the surgical procedure removed the vas deferens portion from my penis, when I masturbated I could still ejaculate sperm. So, this told me explicitly, as I am alive and well to tell it, that there was more to this procedure than just stopping me from having babies. This told me there was a reason for such a procedure, that there would be no more babies who would come out of my partner's womb, tainted forever. The government of the United States made the decision that I was a tainted white person and that they would stop me from producing other tainted individuals who would drain our American system from progressing like it wanted to do in the future days. Quite a statement on their behalf, isn't it?

Helen Robinson was another friend of mine at Texas Tech. One of my fraternity brothers was her brother and he would set me up with her after inviting me to have dinner with him and his family after a church service one Sunday morning. Helen's father was the pastor of the church. We met and had a relationship, basically involving sex. She was still attending high school when I was a college junior. Even when I went home to Houston for the summer months and I returned in the fall to Lubbock, we got together. She had long, blond hair. She wanted to be a nurse someday, like her mother. Unexpectedly, something happened to our relationship one day on a trip to Austin, Texas. We got together by happenstance, I would say, not planned, as it were, and when I was accosted by a fraternity brother who said he wanted her more than I did, in no certain words, loved her more than I did, then, he actually challenged to fight me for her. It was Sunday morning too, right before church started. The game I attended the night before was the Texas, Texas Tech football game that I was responsible for covering for the newspaper back home, The University Daily. They all got together for Sunday morning breakfast. I realized I had just been taken on a ride by Helen who had taken a baby with her up the stairs of an apartment. The night was very dark, and she took me in a car to a place I wasn't sure of. She said, "I want to show you something." I smelled a rat, of course. And, I was scared to death because it was so dark and this was an eerie feeling. I had always wondered if I had actually produced a real baby when I would ejaculate inside her, one time only, however. I actually warned her to buy birth control pills if we were going to continue this relationship.

I can still recall a friend of mine, when his dog in the back yard of his house would yelp and cry. I could hear him whimpering. My friend would tell me he yelped and whimpered like that because he missed his mother. This was primarily the reason why the Baytown Police Department pulled me over. To tell me that I had used the same words to the pastor that my friend had used to describe why his dog was crying. The pastor of the church thought I was designing something bad against him and members of the church by virtue of telling him his mother might be crying for him after the way he and his church had treated me. I came to apply for an open spot for minister of music. I became frustrated. I sent the last email to him because he and his assistant would not answer me and they did not intend on hiring me, I later deduced. So, the police were alerted from the preacher I sent these emails to, and ordered me to stay clear of the church and to not send any more emails to him or to his staff. They did hire a new music director even before the six-month deadline had passed to select one. They declared me ineligible two months before the deadline had passed. And, they hired the new one on approximately the exact date as the six-month deadline had come.

In one of his first sermons Reverend Piatt would give, he told the congregation that years previously in Baytown, that people would be murdered who were strangers in their town.

Sylvester says he knows the game. He plays by the rules of the game. He walks around with his cane like he is going to use it. It would certainly be boring around here without him around to entertain us.

Someone stole the Indian ladies' pepper shaker she brought into the lunchroom for everyone's use. Guess what? This occurred the following night after I gave my seat up for Gracie to sit and eat her dinner. And, I offered my seat because there were no remaining seats anywhere. I took my place standing up to wait for dinner. This Indian lady could be heard making soft soothing sighs of sympathy towards me as I sat waiting on dinner. I ate standing up and I left my plate behind me and walked out. I did not wait for water to be served.

Sylvester was one who told me I would not get water in the lunchroom again. Also, Sylvester said that if I was going by myself, and where that was, only Sylvester would know, then, I should not say another word to him nor anyone else.

One more thing, my winter red beanie cap came up missing today at the library, of all places. I am suspecting two, even more, black people there. And, the hit man was as big as a refrigerator and I was gay, in their eyes. Perfect alibis, perfect caper. Too much reproach. The counter lady took money from me once before and thought I would forget it. She was the kingpin in stealing my cap, I presume. Rest assured. I don't have a telephone to file a police report.

One law for everybody. One voice for all. I wonder if laws are there to protect most people The U.S. Constitution was signed to give protection to. There would be some who would be left out of this protection and the benefits for it. It is not a document that is all inclusive. It has holes in it all over the place. That is why it is a document that is no longer trusted. If a person thinks a different way, he is labeled a traitor. He is condemned for beliefs he held strongly to his death. I didn't care about the rights I attained as a citizen of this country when they were soon taken away from me. I was sick because I was born to become sick someday. By the will of God, who came to save me from destruction and the hand of Satan. From pre-natal days, Satan interfered with God's perfect will, but God reversed the process.

What, then, is the cause for these murders in our land? I will tell you, it is not due to people killing children because they hate children. No, it is because adults, who are the parents of children, encourage their children to dislike anybody else who is different from them. An outcast, are they not children of God, too? Yet, people treat outcasts like outcasts. Worse and worse it gets. Is this love for your neighbor? God loves all of His created order from man to beast, to fowl, to fish, to creeping things. None will He turn away. None will He label hopeless. The words these killers have uttered, kill and maim just as if they were bullets from a gun. What people forget as quickly as falling asleep at night is what impression they may have left on that person who was indifferent to them. And, wake up the next day, and ask how could someone kill innocent people. Like they had nothing to do with how someone viewed their rejection of them. And, accuse them of taking things too darn seriously. Life is not a game. Love is not a game. Pride kills. There is no love in pride.

Stealing is still wrong. So, is murder. If someone says to me, "for 10 dollars I will satisfy your every longing, and fantasy." And, I have had people give this offer to me before, several times before. Like, it is ordered by the doctor. They promise me the moon and the galaxy for 10 dollars. Cash only, please. No receipts given for it either. It is not guaranteed satisfaction or your money back, either. Just the opposite is true when ladies get together. I use that term, lady, loosely here. Do people have to be drunk with wine to have fornication? No one can engage in a sexual encounter without a kick? Even in simulation of the act? Using only your imagination?

Is this also sinful, I ask you? When no one has a partner, is it considered adultery, to look on a woman, without also lusting for her? For shame it is, to accuse me by saying God has turned me over in my lust for sex. They are concerned with the causes for an addiction. When, it wasn't an addiction at all in the first place. Now preachers refer to it as a habit. Some Bible teachers even refer to it as a problem that endangers the process of God's perfect will. Even claiming that I endorse mass murderers who kill innocent children. And, if I agree with that proposition, then, I am no longer welcome in the audience. All I said was, that these nutcases Dr. Ed Young proposed are guilty of these mass murders goes hand-in-hand with previous killings of people who treat people differently. I said the reason why nutcases come to kill is because of the rejection they feel by living in this society. And, it is real rejection. I don't endorse killing anybody, nor have I done so or even seriously given it much thought. It is the people who treat people like me as if we were second-class citizens that enables us to seek justice for ideas placed in our heads by so-called normal people. When no one defends you against charges leveled against you, the alternative is to lash out and defend yourself.

Marie asked if I knew that Kelly had been in the military. I said yes, I knew that. It was another way to say Miss Kelly was a strong person. She followed through on her military assignment, whereas, I got chased off of mine. To be yellow, and also known as yellow, for a man, and then told I was not man enough, is a put down of my character as a Christian and a man.

Which brings us to gays in the military, doesn't it? Bill Clinton inserted the phrase, "don't ask, don't tell," into our jargon. President

Clinton said, restitution needs to be paid, in money, as well as, recognition, to our black neighbors, whom we enslaved when we set up our country. He said, we should all say we are sorry we made them slaves. Clinton said all of us are responsible and should own up to our participation in making them slaves.

When Miss Marie and Miss Kelley denied me food for dinner, was this justice? Like, Texas justice?

Because they both were smiling from ear to ear, while at the same time, refusing to hear the anger in my voice and my complaint.

By the way, can you tell me what this justice was for? Can you please tell me that? I really never got the pronouncement on the reason(s).

Oh, another thing kind of rocks my boat, too. Where on earth is it legal to continue to threaten the life of another person, or resident, and not receive a warrant for his arrest? Until he carries his threats out? Some more justice for you? Even the first charge on why I was held out of the lunchroom, was never fully resolved.

I have a very good memory of these incidents, and what, if anything has been done to hammer out a resolution of them? I look up and I see justice resembling, not justice for me, but for them only.

Jesus loves you. People have questioned my salvation. Being born tainted has never been a strong suit for me, and I don't encourage it.

Miss Marie and Miss Kelley denied me food for dinner.

On purpose, to make me mad, the staff denied me water, any kind of drink, and said, in their defense, "I forgot," and, "you are in a group of 20 or more persons we have to serve every day, "so, you are not so special to require water every day when so many require much more to survive than you do. You ought to be grateful.

Some people push my buttons to test my patience, and when I show my anger, they insist I need to ask for more patience from God. Obviously, God isn't helping me at all, they think. We are not in touch, so they say of me and God. Like I should read the book on dining ethics and etiquette, class entry level 101 to refresh my memory on how to ask politely the server for my daily sustenance. And, then, leave me at the table alone stupefied as to where they went, like I am invisible to them now, not there anymore in their sight. I am perfectly aware of where I am, waiting for my water after my meal. Where is justice for me? Where is the fairness for all, equally distributed? This is a double standard the staff was pulling off.

Galatians 5:26 tells us, "Let us not be desirous of vain glory, provoking one another, envying one another." But, rather, confessing our sins, one with another, not judging, but accepting and forgiving, and desiring to pray for one another in our despair and in our rejections. If we claim we are Christians, then, it is an obligation to support one another in our hurts and in our pain, not retaliating against each other and seeking selfish ambitions. The Bible is not a book on telling us how to get along with people. And, it is only for those who find it difficult to do so. This is a fallacy among people who think so highly of themselves, that they don't have to pick it up because they know all about it. "We know Jesus, we know Him. What is the big deal? Anyway.

Huh, they insist. Life is not about pleasing Jesus or God, but getting as much love as you can stand. Jesus and God kill a good time." Maybe, this is why I find it hard to believe I am liked by anybody. Among our churches today, believers espouse they know Jesus Christ and do not pick up a Bible at all. They have the idea they are too good to and better than those who "have to" read it to understand what life is all about. In utter humility of spirit and soul, real bona-fide Christians show their worth by remaining faithful to their calling. We do not wane or waver to the left or to the right, but we let go and let God direct our steps and our thoughts.

(II Timothy, 2:21) If a man therefore, purges himself from these, he shall be a vessel unto honor, sanctified, and meet for the master's use, and prepared unto every good work.

Marie didn't forget to serve me my drink. She simply planned not to do so by the suggesting of Mark and the other members of the staff. Is not this the blind leading the blind into a ditch, like an addict who needs his next fix? They needed a little push first. Well, it has been almost 20 years ago, June 6, 1996, that I quit drinking for the final time. And, even an earlier date for all drugs, including marijuana. I quit nicotine after Osama Bin Laden carried out the twin tower killings in 2001, following the death of Peter Jennings, the newsman for ABC, who died of lung cancer following the 9/11 bombings. That has been some 14 years ago.

Neither of the staff members has done anything that I have not done myself. What does this tell me about the manager? He doesn't respect his elders.

I drove my car somewhere every day while I was a resident at Dee's Halfway House. For service to Dee's Halfway House, I never once received a dime. I was there for 12 long years. She would send me places I had never before been in the city of Houston, and all I had was a memory to rely on to get to the places she would tell me to drive to. I relied on it continuously, and it usually never let me down.

A white van came to pick me up to take my belongings to the halfway house. I drove my 1978 Cutlass Supreme, following the van driver to the southwest side of Houston. I was not aware of what I would find or what I was to be doing there. A complete mystery it was to me from the time I left my apartment in north Houston to Dee's place, all the way over on the other side of town. She sent me to the Social Security office, chaperoned by her assistant, after a short stay. They issued a check to me every month, addressed to my payee, my dad, Dwight Moorhead. I never knew the amount, but my rent was included in the amount my dad would send to Miss Dee every month. I would get two cigarettes, once in the morning after breakfast, and two more after supper in the evening. While others received some petty cash to spend during the day, I did not receive any money for the first 10 years of my residency there. Then, Miss Dee would give me a three-dollar allowance, throwing in a whole pack of cigarettes.

I took the bus downtown to finish my certificate at Barclay Career School on Polk Street. I would win an electric typewriter for finishing first in the typing contest, with a 70 word-per-minute average. Together, with a final award for the spelling bee, I garnered two medals they hung around my neck. After selling my car, I would be told to drive the daily food run to the stores to pick up our food to store at Miss Dee's property. A pick-up truck, full of food and drinks, I would drive the morning hours with a shotgun driver in the passenger seat. We unloaded and packed away food in refrigerator storage. I picked up food from grocery stores, churches, and Antoine's Po-Boy's warehouse, out in the Greenspoint area where they put the po-boys together. Also, I delivered food for the after-school lunch program President Bill Clinton would inaugurate and put into law for poor children who had only a single-parent. Miss Dee made it possible by having sandwiches put together at the house before I made my deliveries by the auspices of community service workers doing their hours.

There were many other things I did. When I would tire, I would refuse to eat, and Miss Dee would be worried and usually send someone to pick me up and put me into the hospital. My psychiatrist was the one who sent me to her house. They knew each other by prior commitments and worked with each other on many cases, including mine. I had been laid off from my job at Brown & Root, on Clinton Drive, Houston, and I could not find work to pay my apartment rent. I asked my parents if I could come back to live with them, but they said, "no", and said also they could not help me financially.

I changed my medication only once in the 35 years I have taken medication. Sometimes, my doctor would make me wait as long as two hours to see him, even though I had an appointment that day. Then, under his care, I would only receive maybe, 10 minutes of his time, after he came into the room. After almost 20 years of his help, I moved to a different town, and he said he could no longer help me. I came to my appointment one Saturday morning, but his answering service had not made the change until the night before my appointment. I was not aware that the doctor had canceled all of his Saturday appointments in the middle of the night on Friday night. I traveled 30 miles from Baytown to Houston very early that morning. So, I had to turn on my cell phone outside of his office door when I arrived to find this out. I left the building, disappointed, and returned to Baytown in my car with egg all over my face.

I guess I may be stupid after all, a stupid idiot, my older brother would say. He also said I was conceited too, among other things, when I was a little tyke. David had an English racer bicycle, brand new, that never made its way out of the garage. It was black and I wanted to ride it, knowing it was just sitting there every day. "No", daddy would say, "that is David's bike" "He'll get around to riding it." Well, I never saw him ride any bicycle, especially that brand new English racer daddy bought him one Christmas Day. My parents would buy me a brand new Timex watch once every blue moon for Christmas. A brand new Timex watch would always be $10 dollars. It never rose in value, or ever devalued in its cost. Television would advertise the Timex watch as a watch that would never stop ticking, no matter if you submerged it in water for 60 seconds or rattled it in water. And, it never failed to stop ticking. The slogan was, "beat up, but keeps on ticking."

My bicycle was for business purposes only. A rare machine compared to older brother's new English racer. I should be proud and grateful for it. It got me a paper route and I learned responsibility on handling money from customers. I actually had to go collecting every Saturday, door to door. But, I had a buddy, named Dennis, and he was always around to cheer me up. So, all hope was not lost, despite what treatment, or lack thereof, I received at home. I experienced plenty of neglect there at the old homestead, in comparison to all of David's friends, who could be found on the other side of the tracks where all of the rich folks lived. David lived the high life, for sure, while I lived and thrived as best as I could with my alley cats who fought over a morsel of bread.

I played catch with Dennis in the street, football and baseball. But, Dennis turned out to be a track star, a sprinter on the school track team.

My girlfriend, Melba Mallard, used to break up with me every day, it seemed. She would write my name inside her spiral notebook, but cross it out when the wind changed outside. This happened about every 5 minutes. This was Oklahoma, which is a lot colder every winter, compared to southeast Texas. Walking to and from school every day in the cold, snowy, weather, I never saw my brother do, nor can I remember that he ever did such a thing.

I would wave to Melba after school as her mother drove her home from school every day. She would wave back to me, too, as her red station wagon wheeled its way around the corner of the school house on their way to their farm house outside of town. Melba liked to make me jealous, if she could. So, she devised the idea that she would begin to like Dennis McClanahan instead of me. She would continue to harp on this until I would give in and actually make me believe it. This would hurt me to no end. Dennis was not even an athlete. Melba was a cheerleader. But, her plan included, Barbara McClanahan, Dennis' sister, to hook me up with when I got hurt from her ditching me for Dennis.

When we moved to Academy School for the sixth grade, Barbara would come and sit by me after lunch in the gymnasium bleachers. I always would go in there after lunch just to see what was going on, on the floor of the gym. Sometimes, the girls' basketball team would be working out, preparing for their next game. So, I liked to watch them while waiting for class to resume in the afternoon. I was too shy to talk to Barbara, for some reason. Usually, I just sat there, not knowing what to say to her. I was very self-conscious. I didn't like Barbara as much as Melba. I felt Barbara was just doing what Melba wanted her to do. Melba was a very influential girl in those days. She was probably the most popular girl in school at that time, and easily, the cutest one of all. That is why I liked her.

I used to ride with the driver to Friendswood, Texas to load the truck with food from the Kroger grocery store each Saturday morning. The driver was usually doing his community service work and picking up hours along the way. From Westpark/Fondren streets in southwest Houston to Friendswood was a good, slim pickings ride because it brought him a bunch of time. Friendswood was a good 30-45 minutes away from Westpark and sometimes, it would take a good hour to get out there. So, they would volunteer to drive out there and enjoy the time they were putting in, just driving and loading the truck. I rode shotgun, and gave them directions to the store, and dealt with the back-door manager to make sure we got all she had planned to give us that day. She asked me one day if all of this food she was donating to Dee's was going to people who really needed something to eat. Well, I told her, some of it was used for that, but also, I said, some of this food went to the pig man. The pig man was Miss Dee's driver who came to the house to pick up food Miss Dee had gotten from earlier runs we had made during the week. In other words, I snitched on Miss Dee, and the grocery manager from the Kroger back-door discontinued donating food to Miss Dee's. Miss Dee telephoned this lady about the pig man coming to pick up food, and the lady told Miss Dee the same thing she told me to tell her. No more will she donate food to her halfway house. Miss Dee would then tell me, she "doesn't give food to the pig man". I knew she did give food to the pig man, otherwise, I would not have told the back-door manager this. I felt Miss Dee did not protect me or support me in telling the Kroger lady what I knew from doing business at the halfway house for over 10 years, day after day. She made me feel that I had lied on her when she lost this contract with the Friendswood Kroger store. There were several times I went out there on my own, driving and loading on a Saturday morning by myself.

There were times when I went downtown to the Episcopal Church by myself to drive and load the truck. It was in the afternoons, and everyone went on their merry way, doing their own thing. I never got a penny for all of these things, but heartache upon heartache while working for Miss Dee. I dealt with the people who didn't so much as lift a finger there.

One day, I got a ticket outside the church, a parking ticket. They knew who I was. I gave the ticket to Miss Dee. It was for $100.00. I was by myself that day, carrying buckets up and down the stairs to get to the kitchen. Three more stops I had to make, too, along the way at Treebeard's restaurants. Sometimes, I had to stop on the way back to pick up guys from the Veterans' Administration Hospital. I never said "no" to Miss Dee. I never said I couldn't do what she asked of me.

From the very beginning in our relationship there, she would ask me if I wanted to get married. I said, "Yes". But, we never got married. We certainly didn't have a sexual relationship with each other. We never went out on a date or had dinner together. Were we ever really married? You ask? No, not even in the strictest of senses, were we married. She simply manipulated me into accepting the role I was there to do, to work for her and with her. When I would look up, everybody else was having fun and carrying on in pleasure. Miss Dee, I think, enjoyed her people having fun. She would later admit that country white folks were prejudiced, in her opinion, compared to city slickers. I was not from the city at all, as she would soon find out. But, I didn't see myself as prejudiced though. No, just the opposite was true.

I was reading my Bible last night. When I turned to the scripture about the disciple Peter who said to the man with the weak legs and whose ankle bones were injured, get up and walk, in the name of Jesus. Gold and silver have I none, but by the power of Jesus, rise and walk. And, this man did get up and not only walked, but leaped to his feet and began praising God as he, Peter and John, held each other into the temple that day. This man had sat on the porch of Solomon's temple for many days, wanting to enter the temple to worship God, but couldn't. By coincidence, Peter and John, the disciples of Jesus, after Jesus had ascended back to heaven, had come to Solomon's porch that Sabbath day, not knowing this man and his lot. But, all the people knew who this man was for many days, and his plight was well known to them.

Once I had a girlfriend, whose name was Betty Owen, back in college. We met at a college fraternity party. She once told me, I had pity on a man whom I saw had no shoes on his feet, until I saw a man who, not only had no shoes on his feet, but had no feet. She was talking about me, and I didn't even know it. Literally, I did have feet and I did have shoes on, but, figuratively speaking, if you looked spiritually-speaking, neither my feet nor my shoes would be visible. This is the difference in thinking spiritually and in thinking along worldly lines. Peter called this man, impotent. His feet were diseased in some way, and the bones of his ankles were unable to let him walk. But, that day, Peter healed him in front of all those people entering the synagogue. Peter had had silver and gold as a young fisherman before he met Jesus. Peter was married and had a wife. He had children also. But, after Peter saw Jesus exit earth, things for Peter changed. Peter got rid of his gold and his silver and in a miraculous way, demonstrated healing, and Holy Spirit power on this man and many came to know Jesus Christ as their Personal Savior. Peter spoke to some 5,000 and all came to repentance, the Bible says, in one day. We can only imagine what Peter did and had to give up to throw off this gold and silver that was holding him captive and in chains, can't we? I would imagine Peter did a lot of praying on his knees after watching the Savior do the same thing on many occasions, alone and suffering. The ascension changed the minds and hearts of the disciples from that moment on, in doing an about-face in amazement, knowing Jesus was not a Messiah-wannabe after all. There were many Messiah wannabe's, it was said, of those times. They would come and they would go, be crucified, just like Jesus had been crucified. But, none rose from the grave, and none took the walk along the Emmaus road like Jesus did. Only Jesus was able to show Thomas the scars on his hands and on his feet. For Thomas would not have believed had he not seen for himself the scars Jesus had.

"My Lord, and my God," Thomas would exclaim in amazement, as Jesus would tell him, "look, Thomas, and behold my hands, and my feet." He said there will be those who will never see what I have shown you, Thomas, and they will behold and believe. We live by faith, and not by sight, Thomas. "Much more will they be blessed by what they cannot see than by what they can see." This gate where Peter and John met the man with the diseased legs was called the Beautiful gate of Solomon's temple, on Solomon's porch.

I lay flat on my stomach on the back porch when I returned to my mom's house, after spending all of my money on hotel rooms. It was her back porch.

I was once voted as the minister of music of my church. I was only 16 years old at the time. It was not a full-time position where I took a seat in the church office throughout the 5-day work week. But, I was still going to school as a sophomore in high school. Funny thing, my mother and I would draw up the bulletin every week for the Sunday morning services. My name was listed as the minister of music in the church bulletin every Sunday morning as the patrons took their places in the pews to review. My mother and I would pick out the songs to sing as a congregation at home, just the two of us. We would go through the Baptist Hymnal as the church secretary would have time to put the songs in the church program before the services started on Sunday morning. My choir, I would lead also, the adult choir, on Sunday morning, standing at the podium. Usually, we would hold practice on Wednesday nights, with my mother was the pianist, practicing the songs selected for special music. I also would ask others in the congregation to prepare to sing solos for us. This arrangement worked really well for me and the church.

They would offer to pay $45.00 a week to me for this. I accepted their offer, hands down, no complaints. I enjoyed serving the Lord in this capacity very much. I never missed a Sunday while doing this. The whole congregation met one Sunday night after the preaching was over to ask for a vote for me to be their next minister of music. It worked out, I was voted in unanimously. I was more than thrilled to death to do this for my church, and I was very excited for this new role the Lord had prepared for me. I would sing solos myself, too, on Sunday mornings. I sang "The Battle Hymn of the Republic," and "He", "The Lord's Prayer", and a few others.

I came off the disability rolls in the year 2014, of Texas, and the Social Security Administration. I was termed, "able to do substantial work," never again having to prove I was able to work after 35 years of being told I could not. Through most of these 35 years, I did hold several different jobs. One of these was a job I held for 5 years, and I was making $10.00 an hour. They said I was number 2 in a list of employees of 15 people. This was the most I would make an hour, as a result of being put down so many times, and told such a thing was not possible for me to accomplish. I had goals and dreams as a child to become a writer for a newspaper. I took medications that could kill a horse for 35 years. Funny thing, I never knew what they knew about me and my history. The doctors did not bother to ask questions about my past at all. They didn't care about my past. I would have to live with this for the rest of my life. For that advice (sic), they made millions of dollars for the psychiatric association, endorsing Sigmund Freud's advice and the books he wrote that every doctor copied. People who actually loved their mothers is what Freud disagreed with. Well, Sigmund's advice was that mothers were the key to all of our ills and mental problems in our world, even to the extent of accusing mothers, making them the scapegoat for all the inmates in our great and ever-increasing prison system. I say, what a shame, that the medical profession would not only accept this as truth but also support Freud in his endeavor. The doctors and therapists who support Freud in this have blood on their hands. Someone who may think a little different than everybody else? Why? Because they want to be a part of the majority, and they seek a reason to be alive, a purpose. A better purpose for being alive, than all these crazy folks walking the streets. God forbid. Rationally-minded people will continue in their ways, to try to shut off the abstract thinkers. Why? They are jealous and then, angry at those like me who think a little differently than they do. That's it. No other reason. No good medical reason to kill off a portion of the world's population, other than the fact they are different. Do you see it?

Why would Adolf Hitler intend on doing away with the Jewish nation for good? For the same reason as Freud intended to do away with the tendency to adapt to our mother's thoughts. Afraid of losing a great deal, fearful of losing their reputations, their enjoyment of living in the greatest country in the world. Big houses, big cars, dreams to be met and realized. Too much at jeopardy to give up for the sake of the rationally-minded people to look at every day.

A form of genocide, like killing babies before they reach term, as in the abortion movement. The last count was 55 million babies killed, I think, since its inception. Amazing statistic, is it not? And, it is still growing larger every day. The lady who got this off the ground was later converted to Christianity. This is certainly a load off my mind, is it yours? She admitted she is now sorry she ever took this to the court system and had it approved. I said, "Sorry"? You are sorry now, that it is now over? How sorry is this lady? With one word, she has totally been responsible for murders. I say, too late, now to say you are sorry. If there is forgiveness from God, I say, this is not my God whom I claim walks and talks with me every day. Why doesn't she stop it, then? If she is so sorry it happened, then, why doesn't she stop it? She started it. She can end it, too. God is not to be mocked. If it took a miracle for her to be saved by God, then, by all means, a miracle can be done again to save these babies from being killed day after day. If she understands how she came to salvation, then, she also knows how to bring salvation to many more babies who have the right to be born into this world. She took that right away from them when she endorsed it many years ago. With the good graces of the United States Supreme Court, don't forget that. Roe versus Wade made it possible for abortion to be conducted in this country. It had never been done anywhere else that I know of, in the whole world. Except, of course, if you don't include the Holocaust victims of World War II, the 6 million Jews who were massacred in ovens and thrown like ragdolls into man-made ditches. Don't forget the Siberian vacation some 6,000 Russians went on and ate each other up like cannibals. Don't mess around with Joseph (Stalin). My birthday every year falls on the 3rd of January. I got nothing for my birthday from the age of 21 on. Not even a cake was purchased at the local business where I went every day for work either. How do you rationalize that one? I came up with the same reason why the Russians had for running out of favors in Siberia. Nobody cared. Besides, Stalin was Stalin. A man to be feared above all men. This was post WWII. Even Hitler felt the pain of losing the support of the Stalin Russian army. Hitler thought Stalin would come to his rescue to share the pot after the war. Well, Stalin did not like to play second fiddle. He was already a master of the Stradivarius, the most difficult violin to play in the world. Germans made the Benz. The

Audubon is in Germany. Stalin could airlift you to Siberia though, packed like sardines, and drop you just as easy as CARE packages the United States used to airlift to Africa and drop for the children of Biafra. Unusual contrast, you ask? What is Germany called? The Fatherland, right? What do Russians tell us is their land? The Motherland. I don't remember any female of Russia becoming anything of note. Oh, but many we could name as females who have been great contributors to the landscape of mankind. Even England, the great Margaret Thatcher has had her name etched on a lot of silver plates in the United Kingdom. To say the least, Miss Thatcher came after the abolition of slavery. England voted to rid its country of slavery. We all know England has to set the tone for America to change anything as important as the ERA.

England has always been known for its great thinkers and novelists, given the likes of thought that includes Cambridge and Oxford universities. Bar none, the greatest universities of thought in the whole world for everything from the economy to airplane mechanics. England controlled the world for a long time, even the African nations, and as far east as the China Sea. Siberia included. Stalin had murder on his mind from the first day as the leader of the Russian nation. Stalin murdered more people than Hitler did, most of which were his own. They called this cannibalism, eating of human flesh by other humans.

Victimization has been around a long time in the history of mankind. So, has playing the fool. To victimize people continuously over and over again for the same crime, is not good for all concerned. There is a precedent for this and a precedent in place for that person is to say, I don't have to worry about him. He is already been set in stone. Persecution comes with the territory as a Christian. No doubt, the Man Jesus before me, said, they will hate you because they first hated Me. Don't fret over it. Learn to live with it, like a way of life. Expecting it, as you travel along life's highway. I have done my share of traveling a lot of highways. Lonely ones, too. There is not a lot of help when the winds begin to blow and the storms begin to rage. Presumably, I began to think no one cared. When I called, no one came to my aid, or to my defense. Not one soul heard my cry for help. I was too far removed from the daily grind they were all facing every day. The routine they went through every day. The houses they had to pay for. The cars they had to drive to work with every day. I once slept in a vacant house for a couple of weeks where ticks made their home on my arms and my legs. And, I actually went to work every day from that vacant house. It was just a place to sleep at night after work that day. No big deal. I was ready for the call of serving

God from a very early age. This and other unexplained occurrences would follow me. I did do some time, too. For a charge of public intoxication.

Phobias I never thought I had I would be hospitalized for. I had blackouts on the freeway. I didn't have a clue I was susceptible to blackouts. I thought myself as healthy as an ox. Little did I know I was born with an illness that also included a footnote to it. It included something called, the law of diminishing returns. The end result? Death, of course. Dying from a birth defect I inherited. From what I know, it is not only possible this happened, but, indeed, did happen. No way out, you could say. A precedent for something like this was already in motion even before I hit the delivery table. Plans were in motion already before I could cast my ballot. I was too young to demand a full disclosure of the events that occurred that were out of my control. They were non-negotiable too. My birth. Induced? Yes. By whose authority? That is still a mystery to me to this day. If you are a religious person, you would say it could be only one or the other, God or Satan. Religion aside. It is still true; it is either one or the other. Do people have a choice, in reality? Or, is God sovereign in all things? Even in evil. God gave us the right to free choice, did He not?

My birth was unusual. My birth certificate said I was born dead, and then made alive. The box for twins was not checked. Do healthcare professionals make mistakes on birth certificates, or registrars, who fill them out? If a pregnant mother keeps eating, but the baby in her womb refuses to eat, what is usually the cause of this? For a month, my mother would eat, but I would not eat. She did not gain a pound in this fifth month of pregnancy with me. I kicked unusually too hard in this fifth month. My mother reported this to the doctor, but he said not to worry. My brain was unusually larger than normal in my baby pictures. Encephalitis is the enlargement of the brain in infants. Vaccines can cause this ailment. A vaccine of fluoride, a possible answer here. It has become apparent to me of the certainty of a birth defect I have. The defect, I am unsure of, but may include encephalitis resulting from a vaccine that later caused mental illness, and subsequently, I was housed warehoused-style. Post World War II days brought a lot of changes to the American landscape, including fear of losing the title of biggest kid on the block for America. So, why would America adopt a plan to dispose of children who were considered, like me, tainted? Tainted, in the sense of dirty blood. But blood content, like taking unhealthy apples off an assembly line throwing them in the trash can, so none would get sick by eating a diseased apple. Do you know of such things happening in this country, like what I am telling you of? Under the table for a favor offered by a parent to a doctor, willing to take whatever risk there might be of getting caught and going to jail? Have you ever heard of such a thing I am relaying to you here? Does anything like this make any sense to you, concerning doctors taking bribes?

Coach Duane Hunt was my basketball coach in high school. He came from Guymon, Oklahoma where I lived while he was there. He later moved to Borger, Texas. He became the basketball coach at Borger High School. I did not know him personally at Guymon, nor do I remember meeting him. But, at Borger, I became friends with him, where I played basketball from the eighth grade to my sophomore year. After that, I was on the team, only as a statistician.

In Guymon, I played seventh grade basketball under Coach Morgan and I was a starter. My family moved by the eighth grade to Borger from Guymon. In Borger, I went out for the eighth grade team. I made it, but I rode the bench the entire season. My ninth grade year, I went out for the basketball team and made it, and still rode the bench. In my sophomore year in high school, I went out for the basketball team and made it, but I rode the bench again that year. I did not make the varsity team my junior year, so I did not even want to try to make the varsity team my senior year. Instead, I asked Coach Hunt to see if I could be their manager, or statistician. He agreed.

I traveled with the team on road games, but I did not travel with the team to Houston when they played Wheatley high School. I didn't make the flight to Houston for this tournament. In other words, there wasn't a need for stats to be taken because this was a pre-season tournament. It didn't count in the conference standings, so I wasn't carried along. I did, however, keep team stats the entire season for Coach Hunt's team. We finished number two that year, behind the winner, who held a 20-point halftime advantage on us in the championship game.

I always would wonder what the real reason was that Coach Hunt left me off the plane chartered for Houston that year, my senior year. In retrospect, it wasn't because he had no room on the plane, or the money to spend for my seat.

My brother, David, had left Borger High School in 1967 two years prior to this tournament that began in 1969. He went to a college in Houston. He attended Houston Baptist University on a music scholarship. He later transferred to St. Thomas University, of

Houston, following his freshman year at HBU. Coach Hunt knew my brother, for he was very well known as a talented musician, even taking jobs playing the piano. He was very respected by even the home churches in Borger, even the church Coach Hunt attended, First Baptist Church. Coach Hunt knew David's talents well and respected his dedication to the service of our Lord Jesus Christ, I am sure. And, David hit the town running, as they say, staying only one year in Borger, but making plenty of people his fans before he left. Borger was a town of only 10,000 people. Guymon and Borger residents would miss David after he would leave both communities. David would carry this self-importance with him wherever he laid his head. Everybody loved and respected David for his devotion to music. He was a very gifted student also, making the A list, the top 10 percent of his class. He was in all the accelerated classes, Latin, English, etc. He was a soloist in church and had recitals to display his musical talent as a pianist. I thought he was destined for greatness, the likes of Van Cliburn included, a concert pianist known throughout the world. He was that good, and respected.

I had always played second fiddle to David's exploits and this was just another reminder, that I didn't match up to my brother in any way, shape, or form. Again, I was reminded I didn't stand a chance to live up to this potential and reputation that David had established in every town. I was on my way to the loony bin, anyway, and I didn't even give it a second thought that I was headed in that direction. I was headed to my destruction while everyone else was living out their lives in comfort and pleasure. My accomplishments would become nil compared to my brother David's. No matter what I accomplished I could never come close to my brother's accomplishments. I was convinced of this fact.

By the time I turned 21, I don't remember being thought of enough by anybody to celebrate my birthday when it came every year on January 3rd. For, at age 21, my dad would insist this was the date all boys became men. This meant, I was old enough to commit a crime and go to prison also for the rest of my life, as an adult felon. I was no longer considered a juvenile delinquent, but now my dad's motives and goals for me were coming true when he told me this after I reached the age of 17. Earlier, when I was only 10 years old, he told me I was going to prison because I had taken ten dollars out of my mother's petty cash drawer in the kitchen. I did end up in the prison farm years later in Houston, Texas, charged with public intoxication. I did four days and four nights there, locked up behind real steel bars. I broke down and cried the first evening I got there in the chapel. The service started with a prayer and preaching. I must have cried for ten minutes and I thought I would never stop crying while sitting in the pew. There were little white cobblestones that led to that chapel that evening and I thought it was heaven. Out of the mire and into the net of safety I was, away from a society that had again turned against me and pushed me out of their way.

This happened one night in a drive-through burger joint where the police were called to take me to jail. I was the only patron going through this drive-through window at the time this fiasco began. There was virtually no one else on the streets nearby. I got acquainted with two Hispanic girls, not literally, of course, but enough to know they were up to something big and ugly and wanted to take me off the street. They refused to fill my order for a burger, fries, and a drink. They told me they were going to call the police if I kept getting angrier, and they did call the police. In other words, I was not a threat that I can remember, if only wanting my order to go home to my hotel room for the rest of the night. It turned out; there were two of these girls, not just one, who were present behind the window. They gave an excuse about why my order was delayed and that I will have to wait. They intended to do this, to press my buttons and make me as mad as a wet hen. The only thing was, I wasn't showing all of this anger, enough to be charged with a crime and be hauled off to jail for. They told the police I was angry and I would not stop becoming angrier. This was a fabrication of what the real truth was that night. I didn't get that angry to come after them, for sure. In fact, I was prepared to leave and go back to my hotel. But, they told me to wait for the police out in the street. So, I steered my car to the side of the burger establishment like they told me to do. And, I waited for the police to come. They did come a few minutes later and did haul me off to jail without my order in tow.

I remember a check I wrote that bounced in Lubbock, Texas, one day. I received a certified check, hand-delivered to me at my garage apartment by the mailman. I had to pay a penalty for insufficient funds, as well as the amount of the original draft. About this same time at my garage apartment, the Federal Bureau of Investigation came to visit me one afternoon. There were two of them who knocked at my door with badges waving in my face. They had on their coats and looked like bona-fide FBI men, for sure. They asked me if I knew the man whom they showed me a picture of. I said, no, I don't know him, twice to their question, "do I recognize this man"? They went on their way, and told me, if I do see this man, to call them. The man who took my certified check for 15 dollars and the penalty for insufficient funds in my checking account became almost irate when I paid him the entire amount of the check that bounced in Lubbock that day. I felt the same way after my daddy told me when I was ten years old, when I stole the 10 dollars from my mother's petty cash drawer, that I was going to prison someday. I felt depressed and hopeless.

I remember another time I had to call my dad to come and get my car out of the storage lot after I was towed. This was somewhere in the Airline area of north Houston. I was in that area of town because I was in search of employment at the time. My car broke down for some reason and I had to call a wrecker. I called my dad by phone and he came and he had to pay the wrecker to get my car back. He, again, told me to stop getting in trouble with the police. This reminded me of the time he told me that I was hanging around with the wrong crowd when James Jeter's dad said I was the one responsible for his son, who was just out to have a good time. I was out, according to Mr. Jeter, to get his son in trouble, not the other way around. My dad left me there at this storage garage that day on Airline Boulevard, warning me not to get in trouble with the police. I drove home to our house in the Scarsdale subdivision, thinking how much I let my daddy down. We still lived together then, in the same house, with my mom and my brother, Sidney.

I was once in the military, but I wasn't a part of it. I was a civilian, employed by the civil service, working in conjunction with the United States Armed Forces. Downtown Houston was my address to begin working this office. I gave the entrance test to applicants, wanting to enter the U. S. military. I worked four months downtown Houston at the Post Office recruiting office before they chased me off from there one day. I was told, by having looked and studied a document, SF-50, provided by the government document office in New England, that they wrote I stormed off the job one day because I was angry and frustrated at answering too many questions from applicants. They said they sat me down and coached me on how not to become too emotional about the applicant's questions and to refrain from becoming angry, or they would have to let me go next time. They also said, by virtue of this document, which was signed by military personnel, and myself, interestingly, noted I was disrespectful toward the applicants. The supervisor, in his report of me, said many of the applicants would come to his office to complain about me, saying of me, that I told these applicants they were no better than dogs and that I treated them like dogs, too. I was, therefore, denied any benefits I could have gotten by working for the United States Armed Forces in those four months, including both insurance and health.

The money I had left in the bank, the Certificates of Deposit (CDs), I had collected, upon a settlement with my former employer, Central Forwarding of Houston. I would selectively and periodically withdraw, upon penalty also, to house myself in hotels around Houston. My settlement was out of court, for some reason, but I received a $13,000.00 check for a compression fracture in my lumbar region of my back. This happened one day while working for Central. I had use of a forklift in the Central warehouse, and I loaded bobtail trucks for deliveries to make every day from the docks on Mykawa Road. I stayed in several different hotels until my money ran out. This is when I was tagged at this drive-through window at a burger joint and taken to the downtown drunk tank to sober up. I had had only two beers before I left my hotel room. I don't consider that enough alcohol to make one inebriated or drunk and disorderly. But, from the downtown cell, the police took me to the p-farm where the chapel became my refuge from the storm. I ended up on my mother's back porch, face down, waiting for her to come home from work. I was approximately 26 years old at the time. My mother explained to my brother, Sidney, who was also home at the time. "He's sick and we have to pay for it." This didn't sound too good to me at the time, kind of like, is it my fault I am sick now, too? It seemed she was blaming me for being sick, not being able to care for myself, a grown man. She once told me I should be listening. Before she told me this, she also told me that she and daddy always had a good sex life. Anyway, this was not good news at all, knowing I didn't even fit in with the family on social issues like sex. She continued to tell me that dad was raised by an old uncle. This made me feel sorry for him and I should be grateful that I, at least, had a real dad to raise me. My cousin, Pat Trantham, who was a cutie and about my age, once complained to her mother, my Aunt Loi Jean, that I wasn't playing the right way with her one day. Aunt Loi Jean told her something I couldn't hear within ear shot, and from then on, we never played together again. I felt estranged from my cousin Pat after that.

I went to Baytown recently to set up residence in an apartment complex called Pecan Village. It turned out that this was a complex to house child molesters. When I saw this online I was completely surprised. This was after I had moved out of Pecan Village into another apartment complex. I wanted to go into the general population, you understand, and I did accomplish this feat. I could identify at least three neighbors I had had at Pecan Village Apartments who were convicted child molesters. I talked to them practically on a daily basis. I was not aware of this at all when I moved in there. And, I have never been convicted of such a crime as molestation for any reason. This arrangement was made by the Mental Health and Mental Retardation society for housing of Houston.

It seems I was always left alone by myself when my family went somewhere. My dad told me to go outside when he and my family would go on trips to grandmother Rasberry's house in Weleeta, Oklahoma. I was not privy to grown up talk. On one visit to one of daddy's friends' place, I stood outside by the stairwell for over an hour, at least. On a visit to Grandmother Rasberry's house, I went into a wilderness nearby, where I listened to the locusts sing. I must have listened to the locusts for well over an hour until it got dark. It was mesmerizing beyond my wildest dreams, like the Moody Blues would admit in one of their songs. I never saw them in the trees, or know why they stopped buzzing. When they did stop, I went back to my grandmother's house. On these trips, dad and mom would take to grandmother Rasberry's and grandmother Moorhead's house, I usually remained quiet and would not talk at all in the back seat. My brother David, if he went with us, would turn around and fill me in on the license plates of every car that was behind us. Every state he knew by heart. I don't think he even had to look to know what state the plate said they were from. When I finally looked to proof his work, it was too late; he couldn't be judged for being wrong on any plate he saw. So, I quit looking back myself, for fear of being reprimanded by David for even suspecting he may be wrong. I sort of played it by ear. The only time I was allowed to say anything was when I had to pass gas, so everybody could roll down their windows. I couldn't hold it any longer and wanted to stop and go to the restroom. Dad would simply tell me to hold it until we got to the nearest town.

(Psalms 55:5-7) Fearfulness and trembling are come upon me, and horror hath overwhelmed me. (v.6) And, I said, Oh that I had wings like a dove! For then would I fly away, and be at rest. (v.7) Lo, then would I wander far off, and remain in the wilderness. Selah. (v.8) I would hasten my escape from the windy storm and tempest.

(Psalms 60:11) Give us help from trouble: for vain is the help of man. (v. 12) Through God we shall do valiantly: for him it is that shall tread down our enemies.

Satan hates it when I am still fighting to open the word of God. And, I am victorious still.

I never knew, nor got to meet Buddy Holly, the rock-and-roll singer back in the 60s, but I had the privilege to make the acquaintance of Buddy's father one night in Lubbock. Buddy's father was scheduled to make a church visit to my residence one night after I made a visit to his church. He came to invite me back, of course, but as it turned out, it was he who needed help, not me. He began to relate to me his grief for his son's plane crash and eventual death in a corn field. The name of the town was Moorhead, Minnesota. Get the connection here, folks? My last name was then, and still is, Moorhead. I even think the two names are spelled the same way, too. Coincidence, folks? I don't think so. Buddy grew up in Lubbock. I was just there going to college at Texas Tech University. This was my third year there. I wasn't a big follower of Buddy Holly because my hometown played just the top 40 pop hits. And, I only listened to the radio on Sunday nights laying in my bed. I presume Mr. Holly knew my name was Moorhead before he came to visit. He began to cry and asked me to pray for him in my front room I shared with two other Tech students. I don't believe they were home at this time, only me and Mr. Holly. He asked me to pray because he was grief stricken over it and to remove the guilt he had felt for being responsible. He was also very guilty about Buddy's salvation and whether or not Buddy was in heaven. He hoped, he told me, Buddy was, but was not sure of it. He left after this, and thanked me for praying for him. I don't think I went back to this church the rest of the semester, for I feared my prayer may not have come true and I couldn't face Mr. Holly if it had not. I have since heard about the curse that has been attached to the Holly plane crash, but I don't believe in it. I don't think God is that naïve to place a curse on behalf of a person that will continue to haunt someone from taking a plane somewhere. I mean, what was wrong with Buddy Holly, anyway? Can you imagine what his family might feel because of this so-called curse placed on their heads also? Tremendous guilt, indeed. Buddy might have been ill-advised to have taken this flight, but, remember, he wanted to make it big and by his actions that night, was a very ambitious person. This was not his dad's fault at all. I have recalled this evening with Mr. Holly often since my time with him and have fond memories of it. It was a rare event the Lord God put me in, and I am thankful for it.

(Psalms 12:5) For the oppression of the poor, for the sighing of the needy, nor will I arise, saith the Lord; I will set him in safety from him that puffeth at him.

One day while lying down, I was accosted by a regiment of roaches. Calmly, I lay on my bed that day, not knowing I would become roach kill. There is not a listing in the classified ads for employment, nor are jobs needed for roach kill, especially for those trampled by an army of mature roaches. All of them had reached the mature stage, had received their wings. They came through a window overlooking my bed, an open window, streaming down and covering me. I jumped to my feet, and before I could say, God help me, they were gone. I looked out the window and saw nothing that may have brought them in. No foul play. No practical joke that I could find. I will never forget that day. It was the gringo squad, I opined, as Rush Limbaugh used to say on the radio EIB network. I listened to him day after day in my room from 11 a.m. to 2 p.m. on Mama Dee's radio.

I was an avid listener in those days of call-in talk shows, night and day. Even after I left "Reach Forward and Touch Someone", another name for Miss Dee's halfway house, I listened more to the radio than I watched television. After 9/11, I gave my television away because Peter Jennings had died of lung cancer. Then, I quit smoking after that. 9/11 was very taxing on me by media reports. Day after day, I got very tired of it because it was so depressing. I learned about people by listening to radio talk shows. Believe it or not, I was off the SSI checks at this time and doing regular work like everybody else. Making my way and paying my own rent were goals of mine I accomplished over 10 years. I had my ups and downs, however.

(Acts 2:20)) "Notable day" is not the time of the Rapture, but is the time when the gospel will be preached for those Jews who could come to salvation during the Millennium. I remember a time when I was in another town, but I cannot recall why. But, I was sitting on the podium of a church. I remember it was during the invitation that a bunch of kids my age shuffled down the nearest aisle to make a decision that night for our Lord Jesus Christ. I remember them smiling up at me and I was smiling back at them. There was one kid on my left and another on my right side. We were both sitting in a chair, as I was to the right side of the podium looking out over the congregation. However, this was not an unfamiliar place for me to be.

Toward the end of my senior year in high school, I attended a Sunday night church service with my Calvary Baptist Church youth group. Mrs. Parker was in charge of the Fellowship Sunday night after church services. This night, she chose to do skits. We could just make up our own skit on the spur of the moment and act it out on stage. She said to make them funny and entertaining because this was the last Sunday we would be together. We would be leaving and going on to college. C. W., her son, was told he was going to be in the skit with me. So, Mrs. Parker told C. W. to kick me around like a dog and make people laugh as hard as they could. The skit was supposed to bring the audience to laughter. By C. W. commanding me to do tricks, like a dog would do, and roll over, and play dead, and other things. The kids in the audience got a big kick out of it. My parents were not in attendance for this. My mother and dad never attended the youth socials after church on Sunday nights. My mom went home after church. She was the pianist there at Calvary Church. I was the acting song leader for the church, leading the congregational singing while still attending high school at Borger High. So, it was like I couldn't stand up for myself and say I didn't like this idea or that idea. I was under the care of the elders of the church, even though I was a staff member. I still think I did the right thing because Mrs. Parker was still my elder.

I once had a morning to prepare a solo for Baytown Memorial Baptist Church that I had been attending for approximately three years. I enlisted several people to assist in this performance which was scheduled for Sunday morning worship service in approximately two weeks. I had longed for a long time to sing a song, entitled, "Total Praise". Total Praise was a Brooklyn Tabernacle arrangement that I fell in love with, listening to radio station KHCB. I went to the interim music director, Don Thrasher, who was interim because the church was in transition at the time. The pastor of the church, Brad Hoffman, who had been there for eight years, was also scheduled to leave and pastor another church in Virginia. The last minister of music had also picked up and departed to another congregation in Tennessee. So, at this time, the church's pastoral search committee was working to find a new pastor, not a new minister of music. The new pastor search was a top priority over the music director. So, I went to Don to ask him a favor to see if he would let me sing "Total Praise" one Sunday. And, he said, yes, I could. I had been a member of the choir for two or three years already. Don had asked me previously to lead the choir in worship in solo while the choir was singing behind me. These had gone real well for me, I thought. And, other times, Don would ask me to sing a solo. I thought they went well, too, as I would receive many compliments from members of the congregation after the services would come to a close.

One member, a female, whose name was Mary Margaret Myers, told me following a solo I performed, that I had been given a gift. I asked what she meant by this. And, she said, the gift of healing, she said. For her, my song lifted her up, in spiritual terms, as a healing touch for her soul. I treasured her words for some time after this, and still remember how much her kindness lifted me up as well. Her words gave me hope and confirmed I was doing the right thing as God's messenger for truth and bringing the light of Jesus to that city. Baytown was not my home town. I was new to Baytown. I had to buy a CD recording of "Total Praise" in order to play it as an accompaniment. It cost me $50.00. I worked at Wal-Mart, part-time, and $50.00 was a big amount for me. But, this is what I wanted to do. I also designed my performance to include a spotlight on me while I was singing on stage. Where it would be dark everywhere, but not on me. So, the focus would be clearly on my words and the atmosphere of the light coming forth out of the darkness, the significance. After the song, I could overhear Don Thrasher's words, "just beautiful", coming from the front row where he was sitting. This also made me feel very good, that it came from him. Don had a college degree in music and had been in the music ministry practically all of his life. Baytown Memorial had used him to fill in on many occasions prior to my arrival.

I listened carefully to instructions from doctors in the medical field, so I could be as independent as I could, and still maintain a high degree of functionality. Once more I re-entered society as a full-fledged taxpaying citizen. My therapy included ways to deal successfully with distress. My extreme shyness and self-consciousness were always drawbacks and obstacles for me to overcome as my family would move from small towns to extremely large communities the size of Houston. Compared to Borger and Guymon, Houston was much bigger. Borger and Guymon were towns of the size of 10,000 in population compared to the three million in population Houston had. This was a hard adjustment for me, together with my illness, made it almost impossible for me to deal with on a daily basis. In regard to a social life, I was led to think less about pleasurable events and to concentrate more often on things that would be more productive. The medical team I worked, with was I thought, the best in their fields. I never thought otherwise, because I counted my blessings that they were doing their best. I may never know the full value of their support but I do see myself out of a Tom Sawyer novel. I was a rather pitiful person, but I did apply these things I was taught. I was to become a viable member of society soon because I was good and would be a valuable member once I learned how to cope with it. I truly owed a debt to members of the medical establishment for their help. Something is always better than nothing. I had no control over the doctors whom were in charge of taking care of me, as well as all the treatment plans and people who administered to me. I never was given the right of choice of any of these professionals.

My family left this up to God to choose who would be in charge of my healing. For, my mom and dad were also a part of this program to heal also. They had just as much at stake in my healing as I did because they were the chief instigators of what my life was all about. These medical professionals treated me the way God wanted them to. There are no accidents in God's work. He doesn't mince words with his chosen people, like me, but punishes those who get in His way and second-guess His work for His little ones, His Elect, who do fear Him. These medical personnel were very dedicated to making me better along the way. Their concern for me made me a better person and true to God's calling, a gift to this world, like my mother and dad had planned from the day of my birth.

I served Second Baptist Church for ten years in Houston. In the Redeemed Bible Study class, where the age started at 60 years of age. I was only about 50 years old when I was ushered into their class one Sunday morning. I walked into a class where the people looked about my age, in general, young ladies, and gentlemen, but, as soon as I walked in, a guy looked up at me and told me to follow him. He took me to the Redeemed class where these people were much older than I was, I could tell, by the silver in their hair. I had silver too, at this time, but, I was prematurely gray. My hair had changed colors three times. When I counted last, from being born with light brown hair, then, to solid blond and even white at the tender age of 11, and then, again, changed when I was a teenager to brown. Then, when I started losing my hair, and became almost bald, my hair turned gray, and now, at this present time, I have white hair again. So, this guy that looked at me that morning probably thought, by my bald head and my grayish colored hair, that I was too old for his class.

The leaders of this class I soon became a member of, asked me later to attend to their singing each Sunday by leading them in front of the class. I agreed, when one of the women telephoned me one night, asking me to start this practice each Sunday morning after the worship service. Then, after a short while doing this, they asked me to lead the prayer. So, I agreed to do this also. This was a wonderful experience for me. To be so involved in a big church like this, and to do it so well, meant I would be blessed with more and more responsibilities. I had not planned this in a million years when I left the halfway house. Truly, this was a very exciting time for me. I did this continuously for them for the next 8 or 9 years. I never missed a Sunday that I can think of. I was also a member of their big choir.

A counselor of mine once said I had a good parent inside me. But, he stopped right there and didn't explain what he meant. I had two parents. So, if he was trying to tell me I inherited something close to my own parents, then, I felt good about that. I have never been a parent, however.

I actually thought it was John Lennon alone who wrote and sang the song, "The long and winding road." But, I was misled. It was Paul McCartney who sang this, collaborating with Lennon on the lyrics. How and why things in our world happen is an eye opener for me. God never halts His work to carry out His mighty deeds. This is why I have been given life this long, enduring to be a testimony to Him and for Him. God is the One who controls all things in both heaven and earth.

Forgiveness is and always will be the litmus test that separates the men from the boys in our daily walk with Jesus. For most people who have ever lived, from Cain to the last man who will walk this earth, the lesson of forgiveness is the determining factor in how God will respond to you and to me on the Day of Judgment. If a person fails this lesson of life he will have failed the most valuable lesson life presents to us. It is how man reacts to knowing his value and importance, that God blesses him.

It is truly a miracle that God healed me of my mental disorder. With the desire that God implanted in my heart, I began the process of working with Him to make this a reality.

(Psalms 36)

They have no fear of God before their eyes. They are drunk with wine all the day long. There is no concept of God in their minds. A few years ago, while paying closer attention to the ways people judge one another, I was listening to a story that came over the news on radio. A Houston police officer was gunned down by a sniper inside an apartment building in one of the lower income housing sections of our town. The sniper was wanted for a crime already when the police were called. They were there to apprehend him and take him to justice, dead or alive, if they could. However, when the police arrived, they found him a fierce foe indeed. For, he blew an officer away just as the scene had taken shape and the officers were setting themselves. The standoff kept progressing, even after the officer went down. I cannot recall the end result of this story, but I do remember the vigil held for this officer. He had been a member of the same church I attended, Second Baptist Church, at the time of his death. I did not know him personally, nor had I made his acquaintance while we were attending church there. The church's attendance hovered around 6,000 every Sunday in the worship center. The HPD officer left a family behind. I did not attend the ceremony that day, as I was working that day. It was held during business hours.

(Psalms 36:1) "The transgression of the wicked saith within my heart, that there is no fear of God before his eyes."

Funny thing isn't it, when our preachers don't remind us about the tragedies that occur every day in our world. When men fall victim to the seductive power of the great harlot of Babylon. The book of Revelation tells us so. The great whore of Babylon has tricked all men into drunkenness and has spilled the blood of the saints and has drunk of the wine of the judgment of God. God's wrath remains on them to this day. Man has committed murder, killing God's saints. They live to tell about it, day after trying day. They live in denial of their sins. There is not genuine remorse. Sexual sin is designed to kill those weaker than they. As in greed for power over the weaker person, they regard themselves as better than or more worthier than the weak. To prove this once and for all, they involve themselves blindly for pleasure and seek comfort selfishly, pursuing their own lusts to be fulfilled. The kind of knowledge and wisdom derived from this harlotry is nowhere near the knowledge and wisdom one can derive from abstinence and chastity. The two collide and the weaker, the ones who have gained knowledge through fleshly desires, lose this battle every time. Painstakingly, I have been given God's wisdom by remaining true and faithful to God's will and purpose. Obedience to His written scriptures is the only way to defeat the devil. The games Satan plays, he has played since his inception into this world. Like God in this way, Satan also never changes his plan of attack. Satan will attack the weak in the form of the harlot who turns one into an adulterer. He has for centuries, and will do this form of deception for the pleasure of men's souls, for the remainder of time that is left in the world. This is his trump card. He can trick the old as well as the young. Satan has a bunch of successful plaques on his wall to claim as his prize possessions. He can claim he has blinded the hearts and minds of everybody on earth except those who are God's saints. Those whom he failed to seduce by the great harlot of Babylon, he murdered and made all men and women to drink the blood of wine from the goblet of the wrath of God. They were made to become drunk and with the act of sexual intercourse, inspired by the drinking of the blood of the saints, made merry with each other. They lusted after it until their desires were satisfied and still do today. For them, it is sweet revenge against God whom they consider too hard a taskmaster. To stoop so low as to make oneself a slave to the desire of sexual intercourse, they would rage against God's saints. It is not a tragedy and is not a travesty to withhold our desire and control our appetites from the ultimate pleasure.

I volunteered to referee basketball games at my church. I refereed once and got criticized from just those who were playing. This was a church league game. These young men, younger than I was, were giving me the look and the stare. I told someone after this game I was through with this. Angry young men against me. I was ready to quit at halftime, and would have, if not for someone to insist I must stay to finish the second half. After the game, I was too sick to say even good-bye. I simply walked out the door and went home in my car. I was hurt that there was no one to take up for me. Another axiom told me one day on the job, by an older man I worked with, said to me, "Do as I say, not as I do." High achievers say the same axiom over and over. They achieve a certain post to brag on themselves a little to their peers. Through graduating with high marks, they tell other people what to do and what to think. Simply because they have earned this right. The reason being, they have a greater knowledge than other people do, so they reason within themselves. Extroverted people have this innate right built in to themselves, giving themselves the permission to control the less fortunate than them, the introverted, quiet ones.

From the time I was born, my mom and dad took me to church. This is why people would plan to set me up; it is now obvious to me. Unknown to me were these clandestine operations going on, even pointing to the Houston police department to have me jailed, which came to fruition. They schemed and plotted, just like the Bible tells me, that people do all the day long. This, I wasn't aware of, is what the Bible actually said. This is why God came to destroy the earth by the flood. God said he was sorry he had made man, for the awful violence that was in him and how it wasn't getting any better. How people would become angry and kill his neighbor. But, God said, He would make them first, jealous and then secondly, angry. But, this would lead them into destruction, a path He would tell was the path of certain hellfire. I ask you, where did this notion come from? The notion I was homosexual, in the first place? I think people will judge me on this issue the rest of my life, but will also err in judgment when they do. Why? Because the Bible says so. The Bible says they will not be able to judge me rightly, because they do not have the spirit of righteousness. The spirit of rightly discerning what is real and what is unreal. God is also neutral in this respect. For God to actually impregnate Mary Himself was out of the question. He is yet a Spirit, is He not? God is not a fleshly being, to be confused with the mature body of Christ, who roamed this earth 2,000 years ago. He held Himself exempt from doing so, so He could not sin. God cannot sin. God cannot lie. God cannot change. He simply created a way not to have sexual intercourse with Mary, an immaculate conception to impregnate her by His Holy Spirit.

I once had someone actually take me to task on what the Bible said about God. It was a female. She said there was no way God could consult Himself on anything pertaining to His righteousness and His perfect will. Well, I told her, you are wrong about this. I told her that in the Old Testament, there is a scripture that will tell you, explicitly that God said, He consulted Himself. What does this mean, then? To consult oneself? Especially God? Why does God need to consult Himself on anything, being sovereign, as He is? Well, don't we know there is a difference between God's perfect will, and His general will? Of course, those of us who know this is true, testify to this truth. There is a big difference in God's general will and His perfect will. God moves players around like players in a chess game day after day. God controls the chess game too, from start to finish, depending on how He wants it to end. God does this to enhance His name, and to reward His chosen ones. Another word to describe this is manipulation of God. Manipulation is a strong word with usually a negative connotation attached to it; however, it depends on what side of the shore you are on. To be a part of God's manipulative power is in obedience to His word. This falls under the heading of being in His eternal presence, or having a personal relationship with Him. This takes on personal sacrifice and suffering in its wake. This is why pleasure-seekers fall victim to His wrath and His revenge.

People will be satisfied with the mundane of life as long as it doesn't force them to change the way they live. (Psalm 82:5) "They know not, neither will they understand; they walk on in darkness: all the foundations of the earth are out of course."

More than once, I have been told by certain friends of mine, that they like me, except for one thing, they cannot accept. One friend told me, "that is going against your nature," he told me. I wanted to ask him what he was referring to, but I didn't, because I remembered another friend of mine from college, who once told me, "Les, don't show your ignorance." I think psychologists call these defense mechanisms, which are designed to keep us out of trouble by not allowing us to blow up, or, go off on somebody. My older brother would tell me, "Les, you are sitting on a time bomb, here." Maybe, he should get out while he still has a chance; I wanted to reply to him. I used to play mind games with myself about my brother. I wonder if he meant to say, I was sitting on top of an iceberg, and he didn't want it pointing him to the wrong place, just me only. As sharp as a tack, we used to say in school. I hope she sits on a tack; we used to say of our teachers. Then, we could all go home for the day. A friend said I was a nice guy, but kind of "lunchy". This drove me crazy, remembering this like a tape going on in my head. What a thing to say to somebody. Again, I refrained from asking for an explanation for fear of really finding out more. You know, if you ask people how their day is going, they will tell you from beginning to end, and not miss a beat. If I needed a sleeping pill, then this was the time to reach for one, believe me.

This unnatural part of me is so disagreeable to them, part and parcel, wholly inseparable from me that people are willing to lead me into the dark. To them, I am two different people in one. They enjoy the one who is playful and genial, but despise the one who is indifferent. My answer to them has always been the same. Accept me, or leave me alone, pure and simple. The Bible is my guide here on this planet. The Bible tells me my best friend will desert me, and it is true. This is not just a fairy tale or an old wives' tale. When the chips are down, people will run away like cowards. This is why people have taken drugs, street drugs. This is why a friend sent me home half-drunk, one night after a friendly game of chess at his apartment. Who won the chess game? Need I translate? I wasn't Bobby Fischer at the world championships. No, I was the loser, the Russian, who lost the series to Fischer, the American. The world championship of chess was held in Moscow that year. A co-worker invited me over for a game of chess. I ended up on a feeder road off the gulf freeway with a scar across my left forehead. I blacked out on my way home. He gave me a couple of beers.

This is why my older brother would abuse me. He covered it up. This is how I ended up on my back for six months after major surgery to repair a broken vertebra. Co-workers, sold me a lid of marijuana to take home one day. This is how I ended up with a 1,000 pound telephone transformer on top of me. As I lay under it, blacked out and unconscious, my fork-lift standing beside me. I remember looking up at this giant box, and the next thing I knew, the paramedics were on top of me, taking me to Southeast Memorial Hospital emergency room. It was so serious a case, they couldn't handle it. So, they transferred me to Hermann Hospital in the Medical Center because I couldn't move. I thought I was paralyzed, and this scared me to death. I sure couldn't feel anything above my waist. I think God kept me alive for a reason. It was God who actually saved my life that night. I went back to that warehouse one day, off my bed of recovery, able enough to drive then, and went in and told them I would like to resign. And, I did. I signed a letter of resignation at the desk of the manager who went to the same church I went to. His name was Bonnie Duke, a friend of my mom's. I also knew his daughter, being in the same Sunday school class. Mr. Duke was the company's accountant there and had been there for many years. He worked under the owner of the moving company on Mykawa Road, and was a deacon. My insurance paid for my surgery, but left me handicapped with two titanium rods in my back. I would never have the same athletic body I had had before. This was such a blow to my psyche, it almost made me want to die. I couldn't even bend over and touch my toes anymore.

My problem was, no one had ever heard of my hometown, mainly because it was too close to the border, the border of Texas and Oklahoma. There were differences between the two states. One had many more greeneries to admire, while the other was sort of a wasteland, with tumbleweeds.

I was told to masturbate. They didn't understand how one could be made a eunuch in the first place. I guess they considered this, but not to the point it could have happened. In other words, I felt I was accursed for some reason.

I am a cowboy, a son of a cowboy. To be called a man was to me, offensive. This is the cowboy heritage I grew to love. Including the likes of Roy Rogers and Dale Evans, and Gene Autry were my heroes of yesteryear. There is no comparison, one to the other, because I know what Texans mean when they say "he is a good man". Oil men versus cowboys? Look out, you are asking for a fight. I know the heritage of oil men, and I think I got them beat, hands down anyway. The likes of whom? Oil barons? Name one better than Roy Rogers on the Navajo Trail, and I'll debate it, character-wise. From what I have learned about oilmen, is that they would cheat you out of your last nickel if they could, and many have done so. Roy would never have so much as given this a thought. Either would the Lone Ranger and Tonto have thought such a thing. A cowboy is the same at home as he is on the job.

We can learn from evil in our world. Why? How many rich people are there, compared to poor people, like me? What percentage of people in our world are here to make a fortune instead of helping the stranger on the street? They love filling their pocketbooks, not praising my Lord God. Why did everyone expect Seattle to win the last Super Bowl of 2015? Because, even Coach Pete Carroll, it was too obvious a call to let his big running back take the football across the goal line. No, this was a job for Superman, making something complicated when it was so simple a decision. This involved a master plan, in a very short period of time to deal with, and consultants were too numerous. So, I've got to be the hero, Carroll reasoned. He was the head coach of the best team in the NFL, and no one is going to spoil this. So, said, Leslie Gore, too, in a song she made famous a long time ago. He gambled on a Las Vegas showgirl. And, he got the part on his inaugural audition.

King David asked the same question to God. Why are you letting all of my adversaries get rich and me, I can't buy a job, or a lunch. Well, sports fans, God doesn't change, doesn't lie. God is sovereign. He doesn't nap on Sundays like most Americans after church do. He neither sleeps, nor does He slumber. Even King David, the apple of His eye, had some setbacks, did he not? Even murder was on his plate, wasn't it? David did some pretty horrendous things himself. And, riches and money, forget it, to God they are overrated, believe me. It is still the heart God is interested in changing, not your pocketbook. King David, when he murdered Uriah, and then, tried to cover that up, sinned. But, it was for a good cause, he needed another wife. And, it was his day off from fighting the Philistines. A great day to take upstairs to the roof with a cool Corona and sunbathe a while. He needed to rest his bones and his brain from being overworked and underpaid. It was love at first sight. Wow, what a catch. And, David didn't even fish. What to my wondering eyes did appear, but a silver sleigh and 10 tiny reindeer? Smile, David, you're on Candid Camera.

You know, preachers say the same thing today. They will tell their congregations, that there is nothing wrong with having big money.

There is nothing wrong with being wealthy, they will declare from the pulpit. But, the lust for money is, they will go on to say, is sinful. Every preacher will practically say the exact same words too, from coast to coast, in the big mega churches. It is like they were taught to say this in their seminary training schools they attended as young pastors. And, by knowing a little of how these seminaries are nowadays and what they do teach, this makes perfect sense. A love more for money than for God, even in our pulpits today? Sure. "That is just the way it is down here," as Anne Murray would sing in her song, entitled, "Sweet little Jesus boy, we didn't know who you were." "Forgive us, sir, we didn't know who you were."

There is a chance I fathered a baby and was not aware of it. It was because I was given a vaccine, pre-natally that induced mental illness. Yes, it was because I stole ten dollars from my mother's petty cash drawer. It was because I turned into an alcoholic and a drug addict. It was because I was thought to be tainted, and also having tainted blood. Yes, it was because I was a robot hired by the government to do jobs at a very low cost. Yes, it was because I was labeled a terrorist. It was because I was made to be a eunuch for the rest of my life. Yes, it is a culmination of all these things.

This unknown event of mine, whether I fathered a baby or not, does not trouble me now. The fertility test results were negative. I could not produce sperm after my vasectomy in 1962.

I remember it like it was yesterday, the circumstances which lead to me sleeping in a vacant house. I became a vagabond, a vagrant, not of my own choosing. Not only was I sleeping nights alone in a vacant house, but I had no place to bathe. I had no change of clothes to put on. I began to stink as I resumed knocking on doors every morning. I was selling Bible Encyclopedias door-to-door in South Carolina. I was there to sell books. I would find a place to sleep after I did my daily work, so I thought. This was my set of priorities. I had partners who would leave me for better pastures. My boyhood best friend deserted me as well. His older brother would not stay in touch, my field manager then, so I would not know how to contact him. Things were falling apart for me at the seams. I was feeling very distraught over losing these two valuable friends of mine whom I hadn't seen in several years. We were now college-aged young men, not childhood friends anymore. This began to wear on me something fierce, to think they would leave me there alone to go back home, probably to a better place and seeking solace for themselves, I thought. My closest friend would return to his home, while his older brother, would find time to comfort me alongside a lonesome road with his fiancé. She was making a pillow for my weary head with her warm lap. But, after a short respite, he told me he had to go, so I had to get my weary head up and out of the car and hit the road again on foot. My childhood friend would become a minister of music in his church. He studied music in college and received his degree. His older brother actually stopped one afternoon in town to meet me on my door-to-door journey to give me a demonstration. He did this like there was nothing to it. I was impressed, nonetheless, to watch him do this in front of a housewife. My mother said he was the artist in their family. She said he was different from the rest of his siblings. This family was involved in helping me make up my mind to sell encyclopedias that summer. My mother relayed their invitation to me via the telephone in my college dormitory. I told her I would accept the invitation because I had no other plans for the summer.

I didn't even go to my mom and dad's house the fall semester when school let out for Thanksgiving Day. Their home at that time was not far from college, only about a 2-hour drive. At that time, I didn't have a car, so my roommate asked me if I wanted to go with him. He lived in the same town I did. But, I declined. And, I told him if my mother wanted to know why I decided to stay, then, just tell her, "I didn't want to." My roommate drove us to college in his car, towing a U-Haul trailer. After we got moved in to our dormitory room, he took the U-Haul trailer and hooked it to an old 401 locomotive engine that the college used as a drive-by attraction nearby the Municipal Coliseum. This was the basketball arena where the college team played their home games. He would ask if I wanted to go with him to check on his trailer periodically to see if it was still attached to the locomotive. And, I said, yes, I would. He brought his drum set with him in this trailer because there was no other place where he could store it. In other words, he didn't want to have to pay something to store it. I asked him if he wasn't concerned about getting caught doing this, and he said, "no".

He said his dad had attended this university and had graduated from there years ago and now, he was carrying on a family tradition. He could just tell the campus police who he was, and what his father's name was, and he would be exonerated. I presumed this is how he got away with a lot of stuff in his life. Just referring to his dad as the final say so in all of his affairs, which would get him exonerated from a lot of mischievousness. One time, he took me into another town nearby, when he was low on gas, he stopped by to pay a visit to one of the neighbors. I asked him if he knew who lived there, siphoning gas from their car, and he said, no, but he wasn't worried about it. His dad was an oil man, you understand, and was part owner of the oil company. He was simply doing some last-minute housekeeping for his dad, who was home and on a lot of medication, before we came out of the pits to get back on the road. And, by the way, it was late that night, so don't think twice that anyone was watching him doing this. When things got a little boring, he would just take out his 8-tracks and flip it in, and we would jam, silently to ourselves. I had never heard of some of these guys he had tracks on. Donovan? Who is he? I asked. "Oh, doesn't he have the sweetest voice," he said. Donovan. I said, to myself, huh? Is that his real name? I wanted to ask. But, it sounded too stupid to ask that. After all, the picture on his 8-track kind of told me the story. A big dimple on his chin gave him away totally. Or, is that a dimple? Or, a divot? Like, in golf, when you hit your tee shot into the drink, and holler bloody-murder, and someone says to him, hey, buddy, you got to replace that divot, buddy, before you leave this tee. You understand, in golf, a divot, is a hole the ball makes when you hit it onto the green. Even, on your tee shot, there are times a golfer will hit the ball so hard, and get under the shot so low, that his club actually digs a hole underneath the tee the ball is sitting on. If you leave a divot on the green, when you drag your feet and your spikes leave a scratch mark on the green, that can't be fixed.

When he decided to play his drums, he would go to the trailer, take them out and set them up inside our dormitory room. I thought this was a bad idea. Not only was this an infatuation, for attention and love, but he began to play his drums so loud the whole dormitory could hear it. I thought he could have done a better job of finding a place to play his drums than our room. This is my room, too, isn't it, roomy? I wanted to ask. Besides, our room, like all the other rooms, was not so large than that of a small hotel room. And, here he was, enlightening the whole dormitory. And, I couldn't leave this confounded, noisy situation. The door was blocked from exiting, if I wanted to go to the restroom. It reminded me of my dad, who would tell me I had to hold it if I wanted to go to the restroom on long trips we took in the car. This was one more event of authority I lived with. I remember he had this big smirk on his face, enjoying this display of his drum-playing talents. He repeated this several more times that semester, each time, it seemed he would enjoy it more and more.

(Psalm 139) King David, asks the Lord God: Where can I go to escape your presence, O Lord? The answer? Nowhere, King David.

There was a race for two at the track meet in my hometown one morning. It was a city-wide track meet between the two junior high schools, Austin and Sam Houston. I ran for Sam Houston, and my opponent represented Austin. He had the first lane, in a staggered start, just for two runners. As you may have guessed, I ran second, and finished second also, never making up the stagger. In fact, I fell after I saw him grace the finish line. The time keepers all yelled at me to get up, because they said I have to finish the race. I was in tears for finishing second, and embarrassed I didn't make up any ground at all. I had never trained for this race. I was a sprinter in earlier years. I could run a decent 220 yard dash, my favorite race of all. But, a 440 was just too much for me. I wasn't conditioned to run a 440.

We would warm up, some of us, for the track practice every day by running a cross-country alongside the football stadium. The track coach would ask me what event I would like to run in. He asked me if I would be interested in the hurdles. I said no. He asked me, about the broad jump and high jumps. He said, all he has left are the long-distance races, because I told him I was a sprinter. But, he told me he already had his sprinters. So, I just sort of remained on the team as a floater, you could say, waiting for a chance at anything. Well, I got my chance that day he scheduled me in this two-man, staggered start. My dad was also in attendance on the track, to my surprise. I didn't think my dad had a security clearance to be on my stadium's track that Saturday morning, but he was in agreement with everything the track officials were doing. This 440 yard run was put together as a last-minute entry at the track meet that day.

My dad once told me my mom was in heat, or was it the dog? When she would go out of the sliding glass door into the backyard.

I once got my trophies and plaques I had won in high school together to send back to my high school. I got them all boxed up with the necessary things inside the box so it would be handled without much difficulty, or so I thought, by the mailman. It must have cost me 10 to 15 dollars to get this thing ready to take to the post office. It included the right box, the right stuff to go into the box, and the postage I had to pay to get it to the place I wanted it to go. But, when I took it to the post office downtown, they said they could not deliver it without an address. I told them there was only one high school in that town. I didn't have the street address because I didn't have the means to find it. I didn't own a computer and I didn't think I would have to telephone this school to ask them what their address was. The lady taking my package said she had to ask someone from the back room whether to take my package or not. When he came out, he said he could not deliver this package without the school's address. He said, it didn't matter that there was only one high school in that town I was sending it to. My address simply said, Borger High School,

Borger, Texas. And, he said, this was not enough for the mailman. He asked me, do I want to take it back? I said, "no". So, he took it with him to the back of the post office. And, I never saw that box again. I don't know what happened to it. I did get a chance to call this school's office one day, about a year or so later, to see if they had received my trophies in the mail. And, she said, she would go and look. I waited a few minutes until she came back to the phone. And, she said, no, none of the trophies I mentioned to her were in the trophy cases. This was rather disappointing to me. The reason I chose to send them after all of these years, was because Coach Webb told me that the Key Club trophy I had been awarded in 1970 for being selected the recipient of the Governor's Man Award, should be put into the school's trophy case, that it wasn't for me to take home with me. In other words, to him, it was a team effort that had made me the award winner, not my directions on setting everything up. His statement was still on my mind in the year 2002, when I had made the decision to return the Key Club trophy and my other trophies to the school. The other trophy I am referring to was for being named the "Most Outstanding Journalist" of my district, 1970. I had other plaques I won and also a certificate for being named to the All-Star Cast for UIL one-act plays. I had thrown those away when I got sick. I regret that day. All of these awards were very dear to me. I had to be very sick to get rid of them like I did. It was to honor Coach Webb's request. He was, after all, the faculty advisor to our Key Club that met every week in school. He was usually in attendance for every breakfast club meeting we had. I was well acquainted with Coach Webb. He had been my history teacher one year as well. And, this is where he took the time to tell me I should place the Key Club trophy in the school's trophy case. He was also a football coach, a line coach for the varsity. He had been a coach there for a long time. And, he was a Christian man, too. He taught the Fellowship of Christian Athletes Bible Study class and I attended that class. This was some 30 years later, I tried to return them, but to no avail.

I was trying to find a job in Houston one day. I enlisted a chance by filling out an application to become a teller in a bank. So, after I talked to the bank personnel director, he told me I would have to pass a lie-detector test to be employed by that bank. I went right over to the tester that same day. In fact, I stopped in at a telephone booth to get directions to his establishment before I headed out. Houston is a big place. Besides, I was still learning all about how big and wide it was. I did not want to go out there and not know where I was going. I got there and he hooked me up and asked me some questions. It was over before you could say "it's over". He told me in no certain words, I didn't pass the lie-detector test. He told me I couldn't address whether his test was a valid test or not, because there was no recourse for me to dispute his findings. This was a fact, and I could not retake it again to right what was wrong. He couldn't tell me what I answered was wrong, either. This information was confidential. Only the bank and he would be privy to know. I drove home to my parent's house very hurt and disappointed. In fact, when I brought it up with them, I cried out loud in my dad's chair. I must have cried for an hour, until my mom told me to hush.

Prior to loading our chartered bus for Miami, Florida, I went to a night club in Mobile, Alabama. We had just unloaded our luggage and moved into our hotel rooms for the evening. I began to be aware of the darkness that was in this town. It was an eerie feeling I had not anticipated. It was after sunset, and the lights of this town were off, it seemed. I couldn't even hear any sounds of life. Everywhere I looked there was silence and blackness. I thought I would suffocate if I was left by myself in my hotel room. To avoid this, my friends also took off where the going was good, they said, while I wanted to stay as close to the hotel room as possible. I was scared of this dark city of Mobile. I thought I could get swallowed up by it and never make it to Miami for the convention. My buddies deserted me and in a pack together, took the high road like they knew the city backwards and forwards. I thought, for certain, they would find solace in drink and in women. They carried big money anyway, why sweat it? So, I went by my lonesome to a dirty, lowdown night club, full of drunken sots and enough smoke to kill a flock of sheep.

The live band played an old Three Dog Night tune, entitled, "One is the Loneliest Number" that you'll ever do. I got into a conversation with a good old boy with a beer in his hand. I told him I was Pete Maravich of the LSU Tigers. He said he didn't keep up much with sports so he didn't know who I was. I excused him for that, knowing I wasn't really Pete Maravich anyway. My eyes started to tear up very quickly, fighting off the smoke that became visible. I got up and left because I was forced to rub my eyes to see where I was going. I thought, how do these people keep their eyes open and not burning like mine are right now? I don't remember reaching to turn the lamp off in my hotel room before going to sleep that night. But, I do know one thing, I beat my competitors back. I guarantee you that. I don't recall hearing them come in either. I don't think I wanted to at that point. Lord, give me freedom from the storm that is raging outside and in my heart and soul. But, up from the grave I arose the next day, to get on the bus. Miami, here we come, ready or not. Praise the Lord, and pass the ammunition. Narcissism is terrible, isn't it? Hooked on number one, like Wayne Dyer? Or, just looking out for number one? Is there a difference? I don't know now. I was offered a chance to read his best-seller, but I turned it down flat after taking it home for a test drive. It wasn't up my alley, so to speak. It didn't have my alley cats included in the bibliography.

Coach Duane Hunt started this boys' summer basketball league in our school one year. He was searching for coaches for these young boys to get the league going. So, he asked me if I wanted to coach a team for the summer. So, I said, why not? I'll give it a try. I don't think I had ever attempted such a feat in my whole life, so the going was a little rough, but I managed to do alright. We won our league, first place, that is, in our age group.

Out of the mouth the heart speaks. Oh, do they have issues! Terrible, horrible things standing in judgment over pure, holiness of God's chosen people. The things they say and do are vile as the venom of the worst poisonous snake. They are not in repentance of their sins. They are sickening to me and I know they are, to my Heavenly Father. Their hearts are sick to the extent there is no repair. They love and admire their sicknesses. They hope it catches on with whoever can see and hear them. They are bold enough to demand an audience and a reception for even God to behold their venomous tongues. Unashamedly, they taunt God. In love with their shame, they challenge God to a duel. Oh, I pity the people whose wrath God is on. They will surely fall by the wayside and come to their deaths. They love death. Their beds are their graves. They lie dead all night in their sleep. They don't revere the name of God, nor attend to His voice when He calls on them to hear Him. They rise and are sleepwalking in the daylight hours, like groping in the dark. They search for a light but cannot find it. They love the darkness when they have done their evil deeds. They love evil more than they love righteousness. In fact, they hate righteousness, and love evil.

What is your answer to Him? Time after time, He has waited before, and now, He is waiting again. To see if you're willing to open the door. Oh, how He wants to come in.

They have shared with me that they are sorry, but they are guilty of not displaying the love of my Lord Jesus Christ. This is a solemn realization for me as I have traveled this journey with the Lord Jesus. Their pride gets in the way and spoils their fellowship with Jesus.

(Psalm 100)

One day at Dee's halfway house, Miss Dee had a friend who came in, who needed laser eye surgery. He was a missionary from El Salvador. He wore hard-rimmed, black glasses when I met him. He came to Dee's by himself and I was called to chaperone him to the eye doctor. He would never have to wear eyeglasses again after this procedure. The process would take approximately a week's time for him to finish and I would drive him up to the office and wait there until he was through. I looked for an opening in the window to watch his doctor perform it. He was a missionary for Jesus Christ and he worked from a very remote area for families who were poor and needed education. He was there to provide the children with education while also attending to their spiritual needs as well. Transportation to and from his station was very treacherous terrain, he told me. Many travelers would not come to such a place, he said, out of fear that something bad may happen.

I waited. While I waited, I picked up a magazine to be entertained. I read the account of a young, upcoming actress, whose name was Vivica A. Fox. The picture of her gave notice that her name fit her looks, too. She was a fox. She had been a playmate for one of the magazines and she was excited about beginning a career in motion pictures. Now, approximately a decade or more afterwards, I testify I was one of the first to say I knew Vivica A. Fox before anybody else did.

A swallow: a migratory bird with a skimming flight. (ex.) a bird crossing the pond I witnessed personally one summer night around sundown. It was exquisite to watch this bird prepare itself slowly from its perch, and then skim the surface of the pond with its legs. It barely touched the water maybe three times before taking flight just before reaching the end of the shoreline. It, then, moved out of my sight about a minute later into the blue, clear sunset. I thought it must have already had in tow its flight plan.

My uncle Rondall was a pilot. He once took me up in his little airplane, a Cessna, I recall. A two-prop airplane he piloted that morning, before he exited our hometown on his way back to California. He told me if I wanted to learn how to fly like he did, I would have to learn to solo first. Solo meant I had to fly alone, after passing all the written tests. My dad was in the Air Force during World War 2, so I thought my dad might be able to set something up for me to be able to be a pilot myself someday. Uncle Rondall was an Army man. My Uncle David had been in the Navy during the war. One time he wore his sailor's uniform so I could see him. He had a tattoo on his arm. I asked him what it meant, and he said it was an anchor, like the anchor on a ship. My Uncle Rondall had risen to become a major in the army. But, neither David, nor Rondall went to college after the war. Uncle David became a mailman in Mississippi and Rondall went to work for the social security administration. Uncle David liked cars. Once, he drove all the way from Mississippi to our house in Texas in his new Corvette Sting-Ray. It was beautiful. It was pure white with white-wall tires. It was a convertible. I think the convertible top was black, if I am not mistaken. He asked me if I would like to drive it. I smiled in disbelief. He was asking me if I wanted to drive his brand-new Corvette Sting-ray, and I utterly still did not believe he would trust me. But, he was serious about it. I was only 16 years old. I had just gotten my license not long before he came to my mom's house.

There was just the one I saw give a great personal demonstration, for my eyes only, I perceived, of his skills, escaping the wrath of the killer. The killer? What I saw looked like a sea-faring cobra. He wasn't in flight, that I ever could recall. No, he seldom showed his face. In fact, all I saw was his backside. He would never be before my eyes in daylight hours. He worked alone, too. He danced for me close enough to me, to force me to halt my way. I took close attention to him as he watched me walk along the shoreline of this pond. I perceived it as being his doghouse, probably trying to make me scared of him. He was telling me to stay off his territory, his property. He was a poisonous snake, I gathered, with this performance. What kind of poison, I don't know.

There was once a plan in place, I suppose, by a group of people, to get me to admit to stealing a Katy, Texas Independent School District's van. The plan was foiled, however. This was my first case of identity theft upon leaving the halfway house. It started when I opened my mailbox one afternoon after driving home from work. The letter stated someone had used my driver's license number to drive this

Katy ISD van. Whoever this person was, clearly intimated as the possessor, not only of the van, but also the possessor of the license. This debacle they were accusing me of here was stealing and using this van for my own personal use. It turned into a disaster for them, not me. I proved my case.

Something else I would receive in my mailbox every so often were advertisements for new cars with a key attached to it. I would usually toss these aside in the trash can. However, not all did I throw away. I studied a couple of these giveaways very carefully. I had accumulated a debt with credit cards I had used to maintain my job, my car, and food to eat. I had left the halfway house with nothing except the clothes on my back and a 1992 Buick Skylark. The Skylark, my dad would buy on his personal credit card account. This, he bought because my job dictated I needed transportation. By this, I mean, the job and all that was included in keeping my job, made it necessary for me to drive a car. Without a car, I could not have driven myself to the grocery store, and possibly not to the doctor's office either. My dad wanted to make my life as simple and as easy as he could. I had gone to the department of motor vehicles to buy a new Texas Identification card. I carried this around with me before I would take the written test to regain my operator's license to drive again.

Why would Joseph Benson tell me that a white van would come to pick me up to take me to the personal care home? Mr. Benson was my case manager, in charge of getting me off the homeless list of Houston. The van I used at Texas Tech University to go to the coach's offices for interviews was also a white-colored van. This was done many years prior to both the Katy incident and the Benson affair. The only thing they haven't accused me of yet is being behind the mass killing of Maryland a few years ago. In Maryland, there was an alert for police to be on the lookout for a white van. Police were tracking it because it was always their first choice for such matters. To implicate the mentally ill first is always the police force's best weapon against profiling normal people. A white van is always the color used by medical administrative staff members to transport the mentally ill around to locations designed for drug and alcohol treatment. The police commissioner of the Maryland Township that was involved in stopping the sniper and his young recruit didn't know what his vehicle looked like. The fact was, the police didn't trust these reports because they were too bizarre to believe. Eyewitnesses of these murders were reporting deaths in gas station parking lots but could not tell where the gun shots had come from. The assassin was hidden in a makeshift trunk of a car where no one would be able to see exactly where the shots had started. They could hear the shots ring out, but not be able to say from where they had been fired. So, the van theory was given up as dead due to too many reports of the same nature that didn't implicate a white van at all. When the police department did finally bring these two villains to justice they found no mental illness involved in either of their cases.

This tells me that, first and foremost, police departments all across this country profile mental patients before they will profile even blacks or Mexicans. Like homosexuality existing in our world, mental illness cannot be proven that it is handed down from generation to generation based upon the gene pool. There is no such scientific evidence of these so-called factual events occurring. None. Despite their accusations that mental illness is also inherited through the processes of birth, this also hasn't been proven to be true. However, the American Psychological Association and the National

Association of Psychiatry has removed homosexuality from the list of causes of mental illness. This tells me they believe there is a gene pool for inheriting gayness at birth. In other words, these doctors are sold to believe such a disaster as being gay is not the fault of the person afflicted with such a horrible destiny. But, those afflicted with mental disorders have no excuse for their behaviors. What do we conclude from my own scientific study on doctors of psychiatry? They do not have a sense of humor, nor believe a sense of humor and a personality much matter when dealing with such serious topics as the mind and its capabilities. The problem of psychiatry is that they studied the brain and its functions, but not the mind, which is enclosed by the brain. I am led by the spirit, not by sight. Psychiatry cannot account also why visions occur. They call these apparitions or illusions. These, they say, are conjured up by the will of the patient. This is why they don't recognize or agree with the concept of visions or their existence or the existence of God.

I have been blessed by God with visions and dreams alike over the course of my lifetime. God revealed one more explicit claim of His blessed favor on me by letting me be a viewer of one more vision. In the year of 1983-84, my imagination was put to the awareness of a dark day in a church on Sunday. By dark, I mean, I saw only a few lights that were shining. I was sitting quietly in my place; situated behind the stage that I perceived was a pulpit. The entire building was dark, except for these very few, sparsely separated lights. I could not see anyone, nor could I hear anything coming from this auditorium. I began to rehearse over and over again the message of this vision. I recognized it surely as a gift, first and foremost, for it had ruled out my focus on what I was doing at that moment. I was sitting at my desk that was against the wall. I was staring at the wall, looking up, at the time this vision appeared to me. I was at work. I was in my cubicle that day, reading a book. I had a poster overlooking my desk that read, "Let it snow." It was a poster with a picture showing real snow falling from the sky. I thought it was beautiful because it reminded me of my home. I bought it and I liked it so much that I brought it with me to work to mount on my wall. It was winter time when this vision appeared.

The shuttle launch from Cape Kennedy, Florida had come about. It was the flight that never was completed. The commander was a woman. Her name was Sally Ride, interestingly enough. The flight was interrupted by an explosion. I believe it was on the 18th day of January, right before the Presidential Inauguration. All crew members aboard this space ship perished just a few minutes after it left the launch pad. The book I was reading at the time was concerned with helping me stay sober. I recall the very thing I was reading was the process it took to refrain from using alcohol and drugs. This was the time frame and mindset God planned to reveal this vision to me. I always grew to respect astronauts for their bravery and ability out in space. I compared their bravery to the Salt Flats drivers, driving to set speed records. Somehow, this shuttle mission was cut short, but the Goodyear Tire organization seemed never to lose any ground or suffer loss of life of one of their drivers. I understand there is a greater risk involved in a flying machine staying afloat than a car getting blown up on the land. However, a lot of time goes in to prepare for those space missions. Those astronauts carry a lot of education and flight simulation experience with them before they set their feet in one of those space ships.

I was trying to make a last-ditch effort to keep from going back to Houston after completing my degree at Texas Tech. So, I ventured to an employment office in Lubbock to sit with a counselor about a job. I became overwhelmed with emotion, when he counselor asked me why I couldn't answer his question. I began to be despondent that he asked me what was bothering me. Amidst tears that started to flow from my eyes, I told him I missed my mom and dad. He was moved by my tears and was concerned. He told me to go back to Houston and be with my parents as soon as I could. He said he was a blind man but that he didn't need his eyesight to clearly know I was very homesick. He told me that he perceived me to be a believer in Jesus Christ. He said this because he also was a believer in Jesus Christ and could feel my heart breaking while we sat at his desk together.

Psalm 119: v. 78

Let the proud be ashamed; for they dealt perversely with me without a cause: but I will meditate in thy precepts.

The pastor was responsible for pushing me to include the back cover of my phone in the envelope at the UPS store. As a result, the Cricket telephone people are not responsible for replacing it. A third party was involved, my ride, who would not agree with me when I told him that the Cricket lady told me not to include the back cover with the phone. The pastor said, "It is a part of the phone, the cover should go with it." I left there fully not confident my phone would be returned the same way I had sent it.

The pastor said that salvation comes just once. He said it was once and forever. However, the feeling of salvation can be sought again and again.

I became a back-seat driver. I was never really in the driver's seat to drive any lady. I did have my times with the opposite sex, but they were very rare. I must have been with a woman only a few times, as many times as you can count on two hands. After 1974, I was with a woman only one more time, which I can recall. This was in 1984, and I have not been with a woman since that time. I haven't even had a date since 1974 with a girl.

Psalm 119:99 ---

I have more understanding than all my teachers: for thy testimonies is my meditation.

I was reminded of why the author of the book of Mark decided to leave the company the apostle Paul was bringing on his missionary journeys. And, when I recalled this traumatic experience for Paul, I sympathized with Paul. Barnabas decided to take John, whose surname was Mark. This Mark was also the author of the gospel of Mark of the New Testament. I believe also this John Mark was the same person that had the towel removed from his body as our Lord Jesus exited the garden. I believe this same John Mark was also the same person who appeared outside the tomb of Jesus. I believe this Mark, who betrayed Paul at Pamphylia not to do the work that Paul set out to do, was the same Mark who was involved in these events mentioned above. Jesus did not witness Mark's appearance outside the tomb that held His body. However, He was a witness to the towel dropping off Mark's naked body. But, Jesus' purpose was not to bring sex appeal to His name or His personality. Jesus was asexual, not homosexual, or any other sexual category. Jesus didn't fit any known sexual identification category at that time in history or any other time beyond or before. He was not here to do that. Paul wasn't here to do that either. Man-made love is short of God's agape love in terms of effort being exerted and the consequences one will suffer. The sacrifice is greater for one who gives His life as a ransom for others compared to one who only gives one-half of his life to sacrificing to God.

The Catholic Church has added to the Holy Bible as well as subtracted from the holy scriptures of God. The Catholic Church has its own religion and recruits people who fall prey to their traditions. If it isn't the holy version, then it is not the real thing. This means that lies have taken the place of truth. The Catholic Church has taken the responsibility to ease tensions about the subject of child molestations. Making molestation of children seem profitable is not holy. That man is basically ignorant of God. The Bible tells us, there is no one who seeks God, not one. God did His own investigation of this and came up with this fact, not anybody else. God said, not one seeks me with his whole heart.

The Catholic Church has told me I am sick if I so much as forget that my mother went through this cycle every month. So, why on earth am I criticizing females, they ask me? And, they demand an answer for this betrayal. They can, through ignorance, create evil and demand that I assume responsibility for my ignorance. How does one satisfy the other by such a ridiculous hypothesis? I have not an answer for such a pie in the sky, blue-blooded attempt to blackmail me again. There is no answer for evil when it is contrived out of the blue to disgrace me and, at the same time, defend the honor they have. The Catholic Church did not let me ever forget this claim they had made against my very core. Because, in the end, they were responsible for making this claim of blackmail. But, the association was always in doubt because their loyalty was always dependent on truth, not a giant tale they had contrived from the very beginning. Of course, acting on behalf of God, the Apocrypha will tell every Catholic they have this perfect right to send a Protestant to, not only Hell, but to hellfire as quick as the hex they can place and administer. This is as real as the nose on my face. Does the Bible say the Catholic Church has this right? No, nowhere in the Holy Bible are hexes or spells mentioned, God forbid it to be. So, this rite of passage, we could call it, is derived from their very own leaders who contrive this in their Apocrypha. The Bible prohibits this in its very makeup. The Catholic Church's Apocrypha encourages it. The church gives itself, by its own authority, the right to subtract from and add to, the Holy Bible. The Catholic Church enables itself to mingle in the holiest of affairs of private citizens. To fellowship and have my being with Jesus, in what is called a "personal relationship with Jesus." They add to and subtract from the Holy Scriptures in total sin of the highest order. Because of this, the Bible in the book of Revelation describes their punishment as being very severe, so severe as to be burned in the lake of fire with Satan looking on.

Psalm 10:9

"He lieth in wait secretly as a lion in his den: he lieth in wait to catch the poor: he doth catch the poor, when he draweth him into his net." (v. 10) He croucheth, and humbleth himself, that the poor may fall by his strong ones. (v. 11) He hath said in his heart, God hath forgotten: he hideth his face; he will never see it. (v. 12) Arise, O Lord; O God, lift up thine hand: forget not the humble.

In his heart, the violent man hath said, the Lord will not require of him an accounting of his deeds. But, thou hast seen it, Lord, from the very beginning! (v. 14) for thou beholdest mischief and spite, to requite it with thy hand: the poor committed himself unto thee; thou art the helper of the fatherless. (v. 15) "Break thou the arm of the wicked and the evil man: seek out his wickedness till thou find none."

Jess Stiles, a football coach I got acquainted with and more acquainted with when he took over the freshman football team head job while

I attended Texas Tech, was a church-goer, he said. While coaching our high school team, he went 4-6 in only one season. And, his assistant-turned-head coach, Sonny Lang, the following season, went 4-6 also. They failed to bring a winning tradition back to Borger High School. I attended school there from 1967-1970. The same school had reached the state 4A class championship game in 1962 against Brackenridge High School of San Antonio, but lost that game to Warren McVea and the rest of the Brackenridge squad. McVea went on to attend the University of Houston on a football scholarship and became a wide receiver All-American. He soon made the NFL highlight reels also after graduating from UH. Gene Mayfield coached that same Borger squad in 1962. He came to Borger from Canyon, Texas which was just down the road where West Texas State University was located. This was also the alma mater of Mercury Morris and Duane Thomas of NFL seasons past. Duane suited up with the Cowboys after his WT Buffalo career in Canyon was over. I watched Duane before he became a full-fledged Cowboy. He was suited up in Lubbock, Texas the summer before the 1970 NFL season got underway. Rookies were on display for the entire country to see who the top collegiate signees were. Duane came out in his Cowboy helmet. Mercury Morris went on to run for the Miami Dolphins. Morris was on the team that Don Shula took to the Super Bowl in a 16-0 undefeated season. Their backfield included Larry Czonka and Jim Kikk. Morris was the third back Shula used in that offensive attack. Bob Griese was the quarterback, out of Purdue University. John LaGrone was on that Borger Bulldog state finalist team that lost to McCrea's team. LaGrone went on to play college football at Southern Methodist University where he became an All-American offensive guard. He entered the National Football League with the St. Louis Cardinals. Texas Tech would produce another Cardinal when Donny Anderson signed on the dotted line as a bonus baby with the Green Bay Packers. Anderson was traded from the Packers to the Cardinals later. J.T. King was the Texas Tech head coach when Donny Anderson signed a letter-of-intent out of Stinnett, Texas. Stinnett was a very close neighbor to Borger, geographically. However, Borger was a class 4-A school compared to Stinnett, which was only a class 2A school. Only a very short distance separated these two Texas panhandle communities. Anderson was known as the Golden Palomino. Anderson became a consensus choice for All-American collegiate first team backfield honors as the NCAA leader in all-purpose yards. J. T. King believed the running game still won football games in college despite the numbers many universities were putting up by the passing game. When the school hired coaches in future campaigns, they decided to ditch the running game to go mainly with the air attack. It was a complete reversal of so many years when teams like Texas Tech would depend primarily on the running attack to put points on the scoreboard. Now, after King and newly hired Jim Carlen came on to coach Tech later, they adopted the passing attack and used it as their primary weapon. This still did not get them into the winner's circle on New Year's Day in the Cotton Bowl.

Well, after leaving Di'Jon's, I became homeless once again, being put out in a third ward rooming house. I could not pay my rent on time there so the landlord called the police on me and had me removed from her property. I was headed for eviction at the rooming house I was at, before I was facing homelessness. They forced my hand before I could react in time to settle my dispute with the landlord there. In order to escape eviction, my lawyer's office said I should just agree and go along with the landlord's reasons for getting rid of me and not press my luck on winning my case against them. This forced me to move out rather suddenly. This caused problems for me to hurriedly move out without money to pay rent at the next place.

But, I finally found Miss Dee's home on the southwest side of Houston where we had lived together earlier on in our friendship. And, now, I am permanently settled to finish my book and start my career in sacred music.

Printed in the United States
By Bookmasters